Elaine Walker
Steve Elsworth

New
Grammar
Practice

for

Pre-Intermediate

Students

Longman

Pearson Education Limited
Edinburgh Gate, Harlow
Essex,
CM20 2JE, England
And Associated Companies throughout the World.

www.longman-elt.com

ISBN 0 582 41714 7

Set in Slimbach

Printed in Malaysia

Illustrations by David Mostyn

Project Managed by Lewis Lansford

Additional material written by David Bowker.

Contents

To the student

To the student

Grammar Practice for Pre-Intermediate Students gives short, clear explanations of all the main areas of English grammar, and provides practice exercises for you to do.

There are two ways in which this book can be used:

(i) in class with help from your teacher;
(ii) at home by yourself.
If you are using the book by yourself, use the Index and the Contents list to find the area that you want to study, read the grammatical explanation, and then do the exercise. To check your answers, you will need to use the edition of *Grammar Practice for Pre-Intermediate Students with Answer key.*

We hope that *Grammar Practice for Pre-Intermediate Students* helps you to improve your English.

Elaine Walker
Steve Elsworth

Nouns, adjectives and adverbs

1 Subject and object pronouns

Subject pronouns

I	you	he	she	it	we	you	they

Object pronouns

me	you	him	her	it	us	you	them

- The subject is the person or thing doing the action:
  I *left early.*
  She *went home.*
  We *said goodbye.*

- The object is the person or thing
  receiving the action:
  *She telephoned **me**.*
  *I hit **him**.*
  *We saw **her**.*

Practice

Write the correct pronouns for these sentences.

1 ..*She*.. telephoned yesterday. (she)

2 We watched ..*him*.. for hours. (he)

3 Hasn't .... arrived yet? (she)

4 .... don't understand. (I)

5 Are you talking to .... ? (I)

6 Don't ask .... doesn't know. (she/she)

7 This is Julia: .... have known .... for years. (we/she)

8 Nobody told .... the bus was leaving. (they)

9 Why didn't .... ask .... to come? (she/they)

10 Don't ask .... Ask .... (I/he)

11 .... think .... doesn't like .... (I/he/I)

12 .... asked .... to invite .... (they/he/we)

2 Reflexive pronouns

myself	yourself	himself	herself	itself
ourselves	yourselves	themselves		

- The object is the same person or thing as the subject:
  *I cut **myself** when I was cooking.*
  ***The kettle** will switch **itself** off automatically.*

Practice

Write the correct reflexive pronouns for these sentences.

1 I like to wake ..*myself*.. up in the morning with a cup of coffee.

2 Thanks for a great party – we really enjoyed .*ourselves*..

3 I hate watching .... on video.

4 I'm sorry, Tony, but I haven't got enough money to pay for you. Can you pay for .... ?

5 After his accident, Philip drove .... to the hospital.

6 We don't need a babysitter – the children can look after
....

7 Now, children, remember to give .... enough time to answer all the exam questions.

8 'Should I apply for the job?' she asked ....

9 We're planning to buy .... a new television.

10 He hurt .... when he was playing football.

3 Possessive adjectives

- Each pronoun has a possessive adjective:

I	→ my	we	→	our
you	→ your	you	→	your
he	→ his	they	→	their
she	→ her	it	→	its

Practice

Write the correct possessive adjectives for these sentences.

1 These are ..*my*... parents. (I)

2 I've got .... watch. (he)

3 Is this .... car? (you)

4 Do they like .... new house? (she)

5 Have you met .... teacher? (they)

6 Who's got .... money? (I)

7 I don't like .... teacher. (we)

8 Have you got .... passport? (you)

9 He forgot .... keys. (he)

10 They changed .... hotel. (they)

11 She gave the letter to .... secretary. (she)

12 There's something wrong with .... car. (I)

13 They're having a party in .... garden. (they)

14 Where's .... pen? (I)

15 I like .... jacket. (You)

4 Possessive adjectives and pronouns

Possessive adjectives

my	your	his	her	its	our	your	their

Possessive pronouns

mine	yours	his	hers	–	ours	yours	theirs

- The possessive adjective is always followed by its noun:
  *It's **my** car.*
  *That's **his** mother.*
  *This is **our** house*

- The possessive pronoun is never followed by its noun:
  *This is **mine**.*
  *Give it to Peter: it's **his**.*
  *The money is **ours**.*

Practice

Write the correct possessive adjective or pronoun for these sentences.

1 Whose camera is this? Is it ..*yours*.. ? (you)

2 Excuse me, those are ..*our*.. seats. (we)

3 Is it .... suitcase or .... ? (you/he)

4 Has the dog had .... food? (it)

5 They're not .... keys – they're .... (I/she)

6 I don't think its .... room: I think it's .... (you/they)

7 The police asked me for .... address. (I)

8 Have you got .... pen, or would you like to borrow
.... ? (you/I)

9 .... garden is bigger than .... (they/we)

10 I think this is .... book. Oh no, it's .... (I/you)

11 The decision is .... (they)

12 The cat wants .... dinner. (it)

13 You know it's not .... money. It's .... (you/I)

14 It isn't .... car, it's .... (he/she)

15 It wasn't .... mistake, it was .... (I/they)

16 Have you met .... mother? (they)

17 .... parents say the decision is .... (she/they)

18 .... brother hasn't got a phone, so he uses .... (I/we)

19 .... car wasn't working, so I used .... (I/he)

20 .... house is smaller than .... (we/they)

5 The possessive with *'s*

- To indicate possession for people or animals:
  a) in the singular, add *'s*:
  Anne's bike
  James's friend
  The dog's food

  b) for plurals ending in *s*, just add *'*:
  The boys' mother
  My parents' house
  The ladies' hats

  c) for other plurals, add *'s*:
  The children's friends
  The women's cars

Note: *It's = It is*. The possessive of *it* is *its*:
It's cold today.
Give the dog its food.

It's cold today.

Practice

Rewrite these sentences, putting the apostrophe (') where necessary. If two answers are possible, write the more likely one.

1 We talked to the boys parents for some time.

We talked to the boys' parents for some time.

We talked to the boy's parents for some time.

2   We can borrow my fathers car.

We can borrow my father's car.

3   Have you met Susans friend?

....

4   About sixty people use the teachers room.

....

5   Someone had taken Barbaras purse.

....

6   Something was hurting the animals foot.

....

7   I'm going to write to the childrens parents.

....

8   Jane works in my mothers office.

....

9   The dog doesn't like its food.

....

10 Mary and Pat stayed at their friends house.

....

11 Are you going to the secretaries meeting?

....

12 I put the money in the waiters hand.

....

13 Ians suit was very expensive.

....

6 Countable and uncountable nouns

- Countable nouns are things that can be counted:
  a book, *two* cars, *three* planes

- Uncountable nouns cannot be counted as *one*, *two*, *three*, etc:
  milk, water, flour

➤ Exercise 17: if we want to count these things, we use *a litre of*, *a kilo of*, etc.

Note: *Bread, cheese, butter, information, news, food,* and *money* are all uncountable nouns.

➤ Exercise 14 for *some* and *any*.

Practice

Write 'C' for countable, 'U' for uncountable.

apple	C	cheese		information	
water	U	tooth		butter	
boy		car		sugar	
milk		grass		tree	
table		person		garden	
pen		road		book	
bread		chair		news	
cup		bicycle		bus	
computer		hand		wine	
money		flour		house	

And twenty-two kilos of flour, please.

7 Singular and plural

- To make a singular noun plural, add **s**:
  brother → *brother**s**; car* → *car**s**; house* → *house**s***

Notes

- If the word ends in **ch, sh, x,** or **s**, add **es**:
  match → *match**es**; box* → *box**es***
- If the word ends in **y**, change to **ies**:
  baby → *bab**ies**; lady* → *lad**ies***
- Remember the common irregular plurals:
  men, women, children, people, teeth, feet

Practice

Write the plurals.

brother	*brothers*	woman	
sister		box	
match		baby	
key		person	
camera		man	
church		child	
teacher		secretary	
garden		student	
sandwich		bus	
door		cinema	
lady		foot	
gentleman		boy	
tooth		table	
restaurant		window	
house		banana	

8 The indefinite article *a*

- *a* (or *an*) is used with countable nouns (➤ Exercise 6) to indicate *one*:
  Can I have a cup of tea?
  I've got a daughter and two sons.

- *a* is not used before a plural noun (NOT ~~I've got a sons~~).

- *a* is not used before uncountable nouns (NOT ~~I want a petrol, please~~).

Practice

Write *a*, *an*, or nothing to complete these sentences.

1 I'd like ..*a*.. sandwich, please.

2 He asked me for ..⁻.. money.

3 They wanted .... information about the trains.

4 I'd like .... apple and .... orange, please.

5 They've got .... very big house.

6 Do you like .... fast cars?

7 We watched .... films all afternoon.

8 Have you got .... umbrella?

9 I asked for .... bread and .... cheese.

10 Are you drinking .... milk?

11 I had .... glass of water.

12 He gave me .... orange.

13 Is there .... telephone here?

14 We had .... eggs for breakfast.

15 I like .... coffee and .... tea.

9 The indefinite article *a* and the definite article *the*

- *a* is used with countable nouns to indicate *one* (➤ Exercise 9):
  *I've got two bikes and **a** car.*
  *She's **a** lawyer.*
  *He's **a** teacher.*

- *the* is used:
  a) when a word is used a second time:
     *He gave me a knife and a spoon. **The** spoon was dirty.*
     *I bought a pen and some paper, but I left **the** pen in the shop.*

  b) when only one object exists:
     ***the** earth, **the** sun, **the** River Thames*

Practice

Write *a*, *the*, or no article to complete these sentences.

1 She's ..*a*.. journalist.

2 ..*The*.. moon moves slowly round ..*the*... earth.

3 .... sun is shining.

4 I'd like .... cup of coffee, please.

5 Have you got .... double room?

6 He gave me a lighter and some cigarettes but .... lighter
   didn't work.

7 There was .... doctor and .... nurse in the room. ....
   nurse was sleeping.

8 She took .... sandwich and .... piece of cake, but didn't eat
   .... cake.

9 Yes, I work at this school. I'm .... teacher.

10 A man and two women were sitting in the car. I think .... man
   was Italian.

11 Did you see .... Pope when he came to England?

12 He offered me .... cigarette, but I refused.

13 Did you send me .... postcard when you were in Greece?

14 They had six cats and .... dog. I really liked .... dog.

15 Have you got .... match, please?

16 She sent me .... letter and .... card. .... letter didn't arrive.

17 I had .... cup of tea and .... ice cream. .... tea was terrible.

18 Have you met Sally? She's .... friend of mine.

10 No article or *the* before names of places

- *a* or *the* is **not** usually used before names of villages, towns, streets, cities, countries or continents.

> She lives in Paris.
> We went to India.

- *the* is used before names of seas, rivers, groups of islands or mountains, kingdoms, republics, deserts, plural names of countries: *the Atlantic Ocean, the River Thames, the Netherlands, the Arctic* (land and sea), *the Antarctic* (land and sea), *the Alps, the United States of America, the United Arab Emirates, the Sahara, the United Kingdom, the Nile, the Gobi Desert.*

Practice

Write the names of the places below in two columns, those with *the* and those without *the*.

River Seine	Philippines	Algeria
Luxembourg	Sweden	Rocky Mountains
Istanbul	Oxford Street	St Lawrence River
Pyrenees	Bombay	Barcelona
Chile	South China Sea	People's Republic of Mongolia
Solomon Islands	Hamburg	Pacific Ocean

with *the*	without *the*
River Seine	Luxembourg

11   No article or definite article?

Words using no article

> He doesn't like going to school.
> I think she's at home now.
> I usually get to work at 9.30.
> Do you go to church on Sundays?
> She was very tired so she went to bed early.
> Did you have the baby in hospital?
> Their father's in prison.

- There is usually no *a* or *the* before: *school, college, university, home, work, church, bed, hospital, prison, town.*

Note: We only say *a* or *the* before these words when **the building** is important and not its use:
> It was *a* beautiful church.
> *The* school is very old now.
> This is not *a* very comfortable bed.
> Is there *a* prison near here?
> *The* hospital is closing down.

Words using *the*

> We don't very often go to the cinema.
> Did you go to the disco on Saturday?
> I go to the supermarket every Friday.

- We usually say *the* before the places we visit in a town:
  the cinema, theatre, disco, opera, post office, bank; names of shops – *baker's, grocer's, supermarket, chemist, butcher's; dentist('s), doctor('s), hairdresser('s), toilet.*
  And we say *the shopping*: *I do the shopping on Mondays.*

- But we can sometimes use *a* before these words:
  Did you go to the disco on Saturday? but: *There's a new disco in town.*
  I'm going to the bank. but: *Does she work in a bank?*

Practice

Write the sentences, adding *the* where necessary.

1 Is he still in bed?

   Is he still in bed.

2 Would you like to go to cinema tonight?

   Would you like to go to the cinema tonight?

3 We visit him in prison about once a month.

   ....

4 Can I go home now?

   ....

5 I usually go to bank once a week.

....

6 Does she like it at university?

....

7 School is almost falling down.

....

8 I do all my shopping at supermarket.

....

9 What time do you finish work?

....

10 I went to hairdresser last week but my hair looks terrible.

....
....

11 Bed in this room is too small for me.

....

12 I don't usually go to church but my parents do.

....
....

13 He goes to doctor's regularly – he always thinks he's ill.

....
....

14 What are you going to study at college?

....

15 Poor James! He hates being in hospital.

....

12 Other words with *a, an, the* or no article

> The apples are £1 **a** kilo.
> I never drive more than 80 kilometres **an** hour.
> She smokes about twenty cigarettes **a** day.

- *a, an* when talking about cost, speed or how often we do something.

> Can you play **the** guitar?
> I love listening to **the** piano.

- *the* with musical instruments when we talk about playing them or listening to them. But note: *I'd like to buy a piano.*

> I usually listen to **the** radio in the mornings.
> They watch television most evenings.

- *the* with **listen to the radio.** No article with **watch television.** But note: *Have you got a new television? This is an expensive radio.*

> English isn't too difficult to learn.
> History is my favourite subject.
> She plays tennis very well.
> I usually have toast for breakfast.

- No article before names of academic subjects, languages, sports, meals.

Practice

Complete these sentences with *a, an, the* or no article.

1 She plays ..*the*.. piano beautifully.

2 We usually meet once .... week.

3 I enjoy studying languages but I find .... Latin quite difficult.

4 I always listen to .... radio when I get up.

5 Can your daughter play .... violin?

6 I can cycle 15 miles .... hour.

7 Do you enjoy learning .... Spanish?

8 I take the children swimming twice .... week.

9 I think you watch .... television too often.

10 Did you study .... physics at school?

11 This flat costs £100 .... week.

12 I love listening to .... saxophone.

13 The potatoes are 80 pence .... bag.

14 Can you speak .... Russian?

15 I really enjoy playing .... football at the weekends.

13   Summary

- *a, an* + singular noun:
  We are talking about one thing but it is not the only one. There is more than one of them.

- *the* + singular noun:
  There is only one or we are talking about a particular one. The speaker and listener know which one.

Practice

13a Complete the conversation with *a, an, the* or no article.

A: It's ¹..*a*.. beautiful day today. I'd like to go to ²..*the*.. beach.

B: Yes, but ³............ beach is always crowded. I'd like to stay at ⁴............ home and sit in ⁵............ garden. We can have ⁶............ lunch in ⁷............ garden.

A: But we stayed at ⁸............ home all day yesterday. I'd like to go out. I'm going back to ⁹............ work tomorrow and this is ¹⁰............ last day of my holiday.

B: Well, we could go out tonight. There's ¹¹............ good film on at ¹²............ cinema, or we could go to ¹³............ theatre.

A: O.K. but ¹⁴............ theatre's too expensive. It's about £15 ¹⁵............ seat.

B: That's true. We'll go to ¹⁶............ cinema, then. Or we could stay here and watch ¹⁷............ television.

A: Oh no, that's boring. I want to go to ¹⁸............ cinema.

B: And this afternoon?

A: You can stay here but I think I'll go to ¹⁹............ town.

B: Can you do ²⁰............ shopping when you're in town?

A: Oh, all right.

13b In your notebook, add, remove or change the articles in these sentences to make them correct. Some sentences contain more than one mistake.

1 Our first lesson after the lunch is the geography.

2 I first played a baseball in USA last summer.

3 The Rome is my favourite city in Italy.

4 When I leave a university I want to be the journalist.

5 What time does bank open on Fridays?

6 I often work at the home.

14   *a, some, any*

➤ Exercise 6 for the difference between countable and uncountable nouns.

- *a* is used with singular countable nouns:
  *I'm waiting for **a** bus.*

- *some* is used in positive sentences
  a) with plural countable nouns:
     ***Some** people arrived.*
     *I'd like a loaf and **some** eggs, please.*

  b) with uncountable nouns:
     *I bought **some** milk.*
     *I'd like **some** water, please.*

- *any* is used like *some*, but in negative sentences and questions
  a) with plural countable nouns:
     *Did you meet **any** friends in town?*
     *I didn't buy **any** eggs.*

  b) with uncountable nouns:
     *Did you buy **any** milk?*
     *I didn't have **any** water.*

- *No* is also used to mean *not any*, but with a positive verb form:
  *There were **no** eggs in the market.*
  *I had **no** water.*

- *some* is used in offers:
  *Would you like **some** coffee?*
  *Would you like **some** tea?*

I've got (Wouldn't you like…?)	an apple some oranges some sugar
Have you got …? I haven't got	an apple any oranges any sugar

Practice

14 Complete the sentences with *a*, *an*, *some* or *any*.

1   Would you like ...*a*... cup of tea?

2   There's *some*.. butter in the fridge.

3   Can I make .... telephone call?

4   There weren't .... books in the house.

5   There are .... children at the door.

6   She wants .... glass of water.

7   They don't have .... friends in the village.

8   I bought .... lemonade yesterday.

9   Have you got .... watch?

10   She'd like .... new perfume.

11   We're getting .... new car soon.

12   There isn't .... shampoo in the bathroom.

13   I'd like .... apple, please.

14   The house hasn't got .... furniture.

15   Would you like .... orange juice?

16   I've got .... bananas and .... apple.

17   Did you bring .... bread?

18   I'd like .... water please.

19   Sorry, I haven't got .... matches.

20   I asked the waiter for .... tea.

15   *something, anything; someone, anyone* (or *somebody, anybody*)

Positive

> There's **someone** at the door.
> I've got **something** to tell you.

Negative

> I didn't know **anyone** at the party.
> We didn't have **anything** to drink.

Question

> Did you meet **anyone** at the club?
> Do you know **anything** about this place?

Note: ***Can I have ...?, Would you like ...?*** + *something, someone*:
  Would you like **something** *to eat?*
  Can I have **something** *to drink?*

Practice

Circle the correct word in each sentence.

1   Is there (*something/anything*) to eat in the fridge?

2   There's (*something/anything*) about your friend Alec in the paper.

3   I met (*someone/anyone*) from your office last night.

4   I called at their house but there wasn't (*someone/anyone*) in.

5   Do you know (*someone/anyone*) in this street?

6   I haven't got (*something/anything*) to say.

7   She said (*something/anything*) to me but I couldn't hear what it was.

8   Do you know (*something/anything*) about astronomy?

9   I found (*something/anything*) interesting on her desk.

10   I didn't meet (*someone/anyone*) on holiday.

16   *a few, a little* and *much, many, a lot of*

- *a few* and *many* are used with plural countable nouns:
  *I've got **a few** friends.*
  *They haven't got **many** friends.*

- *a little* and *much* are used with plural countable nouns:
  *Could I have **a little** water please?*
  *We haven't got **much** time.*

FORM

a) Plural countable

Positive

a few	I've got a few friends.
some	I've got some friends.
a lot of	I've got a lot of friends.

Negative and Question

any	I haven't got any friends
many	I haven't got many friends
a lot of	I haven't got a lot of friends.
	Have you got any / many / a lot of friends?

Note: It is sometimes possible to use *many* in the positive:
*I've talked to them **many** times.*

b) Uncountable

Positive

a little	I've got a little milk.
some	I've got some milk.
a lot of	I've got a lot of milk.

Negative and Question

any	I haven't got any milk.
much	I haven't got much milk.
a lot of	I haven't got a lot of milk.
	Have you got any / much / a lot of milk?

Practice

Write *a few, a little, much* or *many* to complete these sentences. Do not use *some, any,* or *a lot of*.

1   There's some food, but not ..*much*.. drink.

2   ..*A few*... people arrived before the party started, but not many.

3   There's not .... food in the cupboard.

4   She hasn't got .... friends.

5   I'm sorry, I haven't got .... time.

6   The receptionist didn't give me .... information.

7   I can lend you .... money until tomorrow.

8   I asked him to put .... milk in my coffee.

9   I've seen her .... times this year, but not very often.

10 We only have .... petrol left.

11 She started feeling ill only .... days before the exam.

12 Not .... people come here in the winter.

13 Did they pay you .... money for working there?

14 There aren't .... towns in this part of England.

15 I didn't drink .... wine at the party.

16 There are only .... people at the beach.

17 I didn't have .... opportunity to talk to him.

18 The bank only lent me .... money.

19 Can I ask you .... questions?

20 The journey was a short one: it didn't take .... time.

21 Only .... students are going to fail the exam.

22 I don't think .... people will come tonight.

23 I haven't done .... work today.

24 I gave the cat .... milk.

25 I don't think I've made .... mistakes.

17 Counting the uncountables

- It is not possible to say ~~one water, two flours,~~ etc.
  Uncountable objects are counted in two ways:
  a) in litres, kilos, etc:
  *Could I have **a kilo of** potatoes?*
  *I need **three litres of** milk.*

  b) by counting the containers that hold the uncountable noun:
  *I'd like **three bottles of** lemonade, please.*
  or by dividing the object into pieces, which are then counted:
  *Would you like **a piece of** cake?*

Practice

Write the correct word for each object.

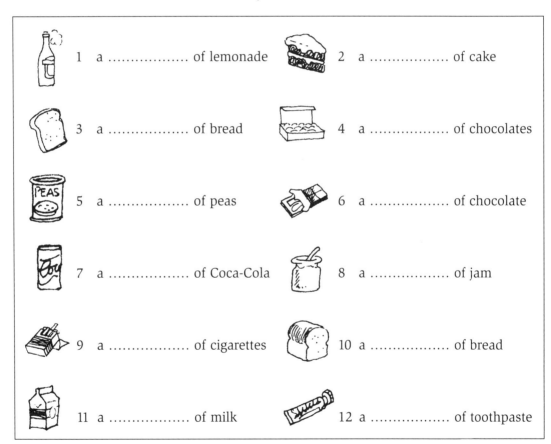

1 a .... of lemonade

2 a .... of cake

3 a .... of bread

4 a .... of chocolates

5 a .... of peas

6 a .... of chocolate

7 a .... of Coca-Cola

8 a .... of jam

9 a .... of cigarettes

10 a .... of bread

11 a .... of milk

12 a .... of toothpaste

18 Comparatives *(tall, taller; comfortable, more comfortable)*

- Adjectives with one syllable (*tall, great, short,* etc.) add **er**:
  tall → taller; great → greater; short → shorter

  Adjectives that end with **e** just add **r**: *wide → wider*

  a) If the word ends in one vowel + consonant, double the consonant:
  thin → thinner; hot → hotter; big → bigger

  b) If the word ends in two vowels + consonant, do not double the consonant:
  great → greater; poor → poorer

  c) If the word ends in **e**, just add **r**:
  large → larger

  d) Note the irregulars:
  good → better; bad → worse

Practice

18a Write the comparatives.

tall	*taller*	large		short	
thin		rich		hot	
wide		poor		cold	
long		young		warm	
good		big		cheap	
fat		bad		small	
old		clean		brave	

- Adjectives with three syllables or more (*comfortable, beautiful, expensive,* etc.) add **more**:
  comfortable → more comfortable; beautiful → more beautiful; expensive → more expensive

- When making comparisons, use **than**:
  Mary's taller than John.
  John's shorter than Mary.
  The big television's more expensive than the small one.
  This chair's more comfortable than that one.

18b Write the correct comparative for these sentences.

1 The Mississippi's ..*longer than*.. the Thames. (long)

2 This hotel's ..*more comfortable than*.. the other one. (comfortable)

3 I think this shop is .... that one. (good)

4 The restaurant is .... the cafe. (expensive)

5 Simon's .... Mark. (old)

6 I think Scotland is .... England. (beautiful)

7 My brother's .... I am. (young)

8 I like this school because it's .... the other one.
   (big)

9 Accommodation here is .... in my country.
   (expensive)

10 The weather here is .... at home. (cold)

11 I think you're .... your father now. (tall)

12 His homework was .... mine. (bad)

13 This film is .... the one you wanted to see.
   (interesting)

14 The journey is .... I thought. (long)

15 This lesson is .... the last one. (difficult)

19 Comparatives

➤ Exercise 18 for adjectives with one syllable, and with three syllables or more.

- Adjectives with two syllables
  a) generally use **more**:
    careful → **more** *careful; stupid* → **more** *stupid; cautious* → **more** *cautious*

  b) but if the adjective ends in **er, y, ow,** add **er**:
    clever → *clever**er**; friendly* → *friend**lier*** (note: *y* changes to *i*);
    pretty → *pret**tier**; narrow* → *narro**wer***

- The comparative of **little** is **less**, and of **few** is **fewer**:
  *I've got **less** money than she has.*
  *There are **fewer** problems than there were before.*

Note:
  It's getting hotter and hotter.
  It's getting more and more dangerous.

Practice

Write the comparative of the words given to complete the sentences.
Add **than** where necessary.

1 He is _more helpful than_ he used to be. (helpful)

2 It was slowly getting _hotter_ and _hotter_. (hot)

3 I had .... time than I needed to finish the job.
   (little)

4 Peter gets .... and ....
all the time. (selfish)

5 You seem .... you were yesterday. (happy)

6 My chair was getting .... and
.... (uncomfortable)

7 We need .... actors for this film. (young)

8 I think that the new salesman is .... the last
one. (honest)

9 This road is .... and ....
the other one. (long/dangerous)

10 Is the new car .... the old one? (expensive)

11 This system is :..................................... the last one we had. (easy)

12 People here are .... they are at home. (polite)

13 The man was getting .... and .... (angry)

14 The city is .... it used to be. (crowded)

15 She was feeling .... she had been earlier.
(miserable)

16 Computers are .... nowadays. (complicated)

17 I think trains are .... and ....
cars. (fast/comfortable)

18 We will have to think of a .... method. (good)

19 I'm beginning to feel .... about the results.
(hopeful)

20 She seems to be getting .... and .... (thin)

21 My new dictionary is a lot .... the last one. (useful)

22 These trousers are too wide. Do you have any that are .... ?
(narrow)

23 .... young people learn to play musical
instruments than in the past. (few)

24 The film got .... and .... until I fell
asleep! (boring)

25 I think that people who live in villages are ....
people in big cities. (friendly)

26 Her new job is a lot .... the last one. (stressful)

20 Comparatives

Check

Complete these sentences, using the comparative form of the adjectives given.

1 It's ...*hotter*... here than in London. (hot)

2 She's ..*more imaginative*.. than her brother. (imaginative)

3 He's .... than all the other students. (old)

4 Do you think Pat is .... than Brian? (intelligent)

5 This school is .... than ours. (old-fashioned)

6 The computer was .... than I thought.
(expensive)

7 The rooms are .... than they used to be.
(clean)

8 He's .... than he was a year ago. (healthy)

9 Do you think English is .... than French.
(difficult)

10 He eats a lot – he's getting .... and
.... (fat)

11 His face was getting .... and
.... (red)

12 He was .... than I had ever seen him before.
(angry)

13 Big cars are .... than small ones. (comfortable)

14 My exam was .... than I had thought. (bad)

15 The road becomes .... after four or five miles.
(narrow)

16 I'm sure I'll find New York .... than Houston.
(exciting)

17 I need to go to the doctor – this cough is getting .... and
.... (bad)

18 He thinks Charlie Chaplin is .... than Mr Bean. (funny)

19 Their plane ticket was .... than mine because
they flew on a Sunday. (cheap)

20 My son is a lot .... now that he's a teenager. (lazy)

21   *as ... as*

- To say that two things or people are the same or equal:
  *My son is **as tall as** you.*

- To say that two things or people are not the same or equal:
  *The second half of the football match was **not as exciting as** the first half.*

Practice

Complete these sentences, using the adjectives in the box.

~~boring~~	comfortable	dangerous	deep	difficult
~~hot~~	independent	old	relaxing	valuable

1   This summer is not as ..*hot*.. as last summer.

2   I hope his new book is not as ..*boring*...as his last one.

3   She was afraid of flying, but I told her it's not as .... as travelling by car.

4   Don't worry. The river isn't as .... as it looks.

5   Silver isn't as .... as gold.

6   Dogs aren't as .... as cats.

7   Our new car is very fast, but it's not as .... as the old one.

8   Do you think French is as .... to learn as English?

9   Were you really born in 1980? I didn't realise you were as .... as me.

10 For me, lying on the beach is not as .... as walking in the mountains.

22   Superlatives

- Adjectives with one syllable add ***est***:
  *great → great**est**; small → small**est**; old → old**est***

➤ Exercise 18 for spelling changes.

- Adjectives with two syllables use ***most***:
  *careful → **most** careful; patient → **most** patient*
  But two syllable adjectives ending in ***er**, **y*** or ***ow***, add ***est***:
  *clever → clever**est**; happy → happ**iest**; pretty → prett**iest** (**y** changes to **i**);
  narrow → narrow**est***

- Adjectives with three syllables or more use ***most***:
  *expensive → **most** expensive; dangerous → **most** dangerous;
  comfortable → **most** comfortable*

Note: The irregulars:
bad → *worst*
good → *best*
little → *least*

USE

Superlatives are used to compare one thing with several others.
They are used with ***the ... in***, or ***the ... of***; sometimes they are used with
just ***the ...***:
*This is **the** longest river **in** the world.*
*This is **the** most expensive car **of** them all.*
*This is **the** most expensive car here.*

Practice

Write the superlatives of the words given, using ***in*** or ***of*** where necessary.

1 This is *the biggest building in* the world. (big building)

2 This is .... here. (comfortable chair)

3 He bought .... the shop. (expensive flowers)

4 I think she's .... the group. (good singer)

5 He's .... the company. (careful driver)

6 Who's .... the class? (old student)

7 It's .... I've ever seen. (bad film)

8 She's .... all the students. (intelligent)

9 It was .... I had ever heard. (beautiful music)

10 He's .... all the assistants. (helpful)

11 He's .... his class. (young)

12 This is .... the world. (poor country)

13 She's .... I've ever met. (strange person)

14 I didn't answer .... questions. (difficult)

15 Peter's .... them all. (old)

23 *too, enough*

- The infinitive with ***to*** is often used after ***too*** + adjective, or ***not*** +
  adjective + ***enough***.
  *It's **too** cold to swim today. (We can't swim today - it's **too** cold.)*
  *It isn't warm **enough** to go to the beach. (We can't go to the beach
  - it's **not** warm **enough**.)*

Practice

Complete these sentences using **too** or **not ... enough**.

1 I can't walk any further – I'm _..too tired..._ (tired)

2 I'm sorry. You're _..not old enough_ to see this film. (old)

3 It's .... to work here. Let's go to the library. (noisy)

4 Ian was .... to get into the swimming team. (fast)

5 Your handwriting is .... to read. (small)

6 I'm afraid we can't buy that computer. It's .... (expensive)

7 I don't think George should get the new job – he's .... (efficient)

8 Those jeans are .... to wear to the party. (dirty)

9 We couldn't talk to each other in the pub – the music was .... (loud)

10 Can you help me with this bottle? I'm .... to open it. (strong)

24 Participial adjectives *(bored/boring)*

CONTRAST

• Note the difference:
  I was bored.
  The lesson was boring.
  It is not possible to say: ~~The lesson was bored~~.
  It is possible to say: *She was boring.*

Practice

Circle the correct word in each sentence.

1 It was a very (*interested*/*interesting*) performance.

2 We were all very (*interested*/*interesting*) in what he said.

3 It was a very (*tired*/*tiring*) journey.

4 We were all very (*worried*/*worrying*).

5 The children are (*frightening*/*frightened*) by the animals.

6 Why do you look so (*bored/boring*) at school?

7 It was a terribly (*excited/exciting*) day.

8 Don't look so (*worrying/worried*).

9 We had a (*tiring/tired*) trip home.

10 It was an extremely (*amused/amusing*) programme.

11 It was an (*exciting/excited*) idea!

12 It was the most (*boring/bored*) I can remember.

13 We were all feeling (*tired/tiring*).

14 Didn't you think it was an (*amused/amusing*) play?

15 The last half hour was a (*worrying/worried*) time.

16 I've never been so (*frightened/frightening*) in my life.

25 Adverbs of manner

- Adverbs of manner are formed from adjectives by adding *ly*:
  quick → *quickly; polite* → *politely; careful* → *carefully*

- Note these irregulars: ***good*** → ***well; hard*** → ***hard; fast*** → ***fast; early*** → ***early;
  late*** → ***late; loud*** → ***loud*** or ***loudly.***
  He's a good worker. He works well.
  She's a hard worker. She works hard.
  She's a fast runner. She runs fast.

Practice

Write the adverbs.

quick	*quickly*	clever	
slow		nice	
fast		bad	
careful		intelligent	
stupid		polite	
dangerous		rude	
good		brave	
hard		early	

26   Comparison of adverbs

- Most adverbs are used with **more** and **most:**
  slowly → **more** *slowly,* **most** *slowly*
  dangerously → **more** *dangerously,* **most** *dangerously*

- One-syllable adverbs add **er** and **est:**
  hard → *hard**er**, *hard**est**; fast* → *fast**er**, *fast**est**; loud* → *loud**er**, *loud**est***

- The irregular comparisons are:

well badly little	better worse less	best worst least

far	farther/ further	farthest/ furthest

Practice

Write the correct form of adverbs for these sentences.

1   She works ..*harder*.. than all the others. (hard)

2   Of all the machines, this one works the ....(good)

3   Couldn't you drive a bit .... ? (careful)

4   I can't understand. Would you ask him to speak .... ? (clear)

5   They all behaved badly, but Pat behaved the .... (bad)

6   John was shouting .... than everybody else. (loud)

7   I think I understand .... than the others. (good)

8   Susan climbed .... than the rest of us. (fast)

9   She gets up .... than everybody else in the house. (early)

10 Do you think they have acted .... ? (stupid)

27 Adjectives and adverbs

Check

Complete these sentences.

1 It was ..*the best*.. driving I have ever seen. (good)

2 Peter sang ..*louder*.. than all the others. (loud)

3 The holiday wasn't ..*as expensive*... as the one we had last year.

4 She's a good student: she works .... than the others. (careful)

5 Would you play ...., please? I'm trying to sleep. (quiet)

6 Of all the people in the factory, Joan works .... (efficient)

7 The weather isn't .... as I had expected. (bad)

8 This is the .... company in the world. (big)

9 She plays the piano .... than anyone else in her class. (beautiful)

10 Mr Jones is .... person in the village. (old)

11 Mark hit the ball very .... (hard)

12 She runs .... than anyone else in the team. (fast)

13 Do you think older people drive .... than younger people? (slow)

14 They all dance well, but John dances .... (good)

15 This computer is nearly twice .... as the old one. (expensive)

16 He doesn't ski .... as his sister. (good)

17 This typewriter is .... than mine. (modern)

18 I think they both behaved very .... (rude)

19 People aren't .... as they used to be. (thoughtful)

20 I waited ....than anyone else. (long)

Verbs

THE PRESENT TENSE

28   Present Simple

FORM

Positive   *Question*   *Negative*

I You We They	work.	Do	I you we they	work?	I You We They	do not (don't)	work.
He She It	works.	Does	he she it	work?	He She it	does not (doesn't)	work.

- There is only one form of **you** in English, which is the same in singular and plural.

- Note the endings with **he**, **she**, and **it**. If the verb ends in **ss**, **sh**, **ch**, or **x**, add **es**:
  He finishes (*finish* ends in **sh**)
  She watches (*watch* ends in **ch**)

USE

- For something which is permanently true:
  *I **come from** France.*
  *He **doesn't speak** Spanish.*
  *We **live** in London.*

- For repeated actions or habits:
  *I **get up** at six o'clock every day.*
  *What time **do you leave** work?*
  *I **don't see** them very often.*

Practice

Rewrite each sentence as a positive or negative sentence, or a question, according to the instructions.

1   I visit my parents very often. (negative)

  I don't visit my parents very often.

2   Does he go to school every day? (positive)

  He goes to school every day.

3   She comes from Germany. (question)

  Does she comes from Germany?

4 She goes to work by car. (question)

....

5 We watch television every night. (negative)

....

6 He doesn't walk to work every day. (positive)

....

7 She plays football every Saturday. (question)

....

8 He washes his car every week. (question)

....

9 They live in Australia. (question)

....

10 They go to school by bus. (question)

....

11 Does she finish work at five o'clock? (positive)

....

12 He goes to the cinema on Fridays. (question)

....

13 I come from Africa. (negative)

....

14 Does he live in this street? (positive)

....

15 He works in a restaurant. (question)

....

16 She gets up at five o'clock. (question)

....

17 They eat a lot. (negative)

....

18 Does he work here? (positive)

....

29　Present Continuous

FORM

Positive

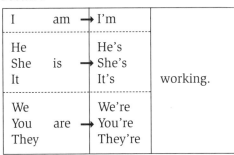

Question

Negative with **not**

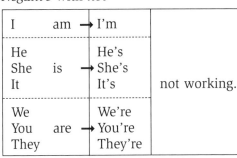

Negative with **n't**

USE

- For an action in progress now:
  I'm reading *a grammar book now.*
  *What **are you looking at**?*
  *She **isn't eating** at the moment.*

Practice

Rewrite each sentence as a positive or negative sentence, or a question, according to the instructions.

1　She's watching television now. (question)

　Is she watching television now?

2　He isn't staying at this hotel. (positive)

　He's staying at this hotel.

3　She's reading. (negative)

　She isn't reading.

4　They're working. (question)

　...

5 He's writing a letter. (question)

....

6 He's eating. (negative)

....

7 I'm not working. (positive)

....

8 She's studying at the moment. (question)

....

9 I'm sleeping. (negative)

....

10 You're reading my newspaper. (question)

....

11 She's writing a letter. (question)

....

12 He's talking to Mary. (question)

....

13 They're not playing football. (positive)

....

14 He's listening to the radio. (question)

....

15 You're playing with my football. (question)

....

30 Present Simple/Present Continuous

Practice

In your notebook, write these sentences putting the verbs into the correct tense.

1 She (read) at the moment.
She's reading at the moment.

2 (You go) to work by car?
Do you go to work by car?

3 I (not watch) television every night.
I don't watch television every night.

4 I (not watch) television at the moment.
I'm not watching television at the moment.

5   We (see) our parents every week.

6   (You listen) to the radio now?

7   I (not get up) at seven o'clock every morning.

8   Peter (talk) to Susan now.

9   (They work) in the restaurant at the weekends?

10   She (listen) to the radio in her bedroom at the moment.

11   They (not come) to school every day.

12   (You work) now?

13   The children (go) to bed at eight o'clock.

14   I (leave) the office every day at five.

15   I'm sorry I can't talk to you now. I (go) out.

16   (Peter and Jane work) in London at the moment?

17   (Mary and Susan drive) to the office every day?

18   We (go) to the beach now.

19   (John listen) to the radio at the moment?

20   (Your parents sit) in the garden now?

21   The film (start) every night at eight o'clock

22   They (not go) to the cinema very often.

23   (You go) into the office every month?

24   I (not study) at the moment.

31   Present Continuous: short answers

'Are you working at the moment?' 'Yes, I am.'

FORM

Positive   *Negative*

	I	am.
Yes,	he she }is. it	
	we you }are. they	

	I'm	not.			
No,	he she }'s not. it		or	he she }isn't. it	
	we you }'re not. they			we you }aren't. they	

Notes

- Nouns → pronouns.
  *'Are **your parents** sleeping?'*
  *'Yes, **they** are.'*

- Positive short answers do not use contractions:
  Yes, I am. (NOT ~~Yes, I'm~~)
  Yes, they are. (NOT ~~Yes, they're~~)

- Contractions are used in negative short answers.
  'Is she working?'
  *'No, she **isn't**'*

Practice

Someone is asking you questions. Write the short answers.

1 'Are you working at the moment?'   'No, *I'm not.* '

2 'Are your sisters working now?'   'No, *they aren't.* '

3 'Are your parents coming?'   'Yes, ...'

4 'Is John working at the moment?'   'Yes, ...'

5 'Are they playing tennis?'   'No, ...'

6 'Are you reading this book?'   'Yes, ...'

7 'Is Mary going to school today?'   'No, ...'

8 'Is Peter listening to the radio?'   'Yes, ...'

9 'Are they doing their homework now?'   'No, ...'

10 'Is the dog sleeping?'   'Yes, ...'

32   Present Simple: short answers

FORM

Positive   *Negative*

Yes,	I we you they } do.		No,	I we you they } don't.
	he she it } does.			he she it } doesn't.

Notes

- Nouns ➡ pronouns
  '*Do **the men** want some tea?*
  '*Yes,* **they** *do.*'

- Negative short answers can use the
  uncontracted form:
  *No, they **do not**.* (this is more emphatic)

Practice

Write the short answers.

1 'Do you live here?'   'Yes, *I do.* '

2 'Does Mary work in this office?'   'No, *she doesn't.* '

3 'Does Stephen speak French?'   'No, ... '

4 'Do the teachers like your work?'   'Yes, ... '

5 'Do you understand the lessons?'   'No, ... '

6 'Do they visit you often?'   'No, ... '

7 'Do you like France?'   'Yes, ... '

8 'Do your parents live in London?'   'Yes, ... '

9 'Does your father like modern music?'   'No, ... '

10 'Does Judy drive to work?'   'Yes, ... '

11 'Do your grandparents still enjoy gardening?'   'Yes, ... '

12 'Does Simon's sister work with you?'   'No, ... '

13 'Do John and Alison eat meat?'   'No, ... '

14 'Does Tony like adventure films?'   'Yes, ... '

15 'Do you watch TV at the weekend?'   'No, ... '

16 'Does your uncle play tennis?'   'Yes .... '

33   Present Simple and Continuous: short forms

Check

Someone is asking you questions. Write the short answers.

1   'Are your brothers working today?'   'Yes, ...*they are.*... '
2   'Do you speak Italian?'   'No, *I don't.'* '
3   'Do you like this school?'   'Yes, ... '
4   'Do you go to school in London?'   'Yes, ... '
5   'Is your mother watching television?'   'Yes, ... '
6   'Do you go to school on Sundays?'   'No, ... '
7   'Are your parents staying here?'   'No, ... '
8   'Does the dog sleep in your bedroom?'   'No, ... '
9   'Do you get up at eight o'clock?'   'Yes, ... '
10 'Is Mary listening to the stereo?'   'Yes, ... '
11 'Does the film start at six o'clock?'   'No, ... '
12 'Are the children playing football?'   'Yes, ... '
13 'Does Susan drive to work?'   'Yes, ... '
14 'Are you reading?'   'No, ... '
15 'Am I reading your paper?'   'Yes, ... '
16 'Are they doing the washing up?'   'Yes, ... '
17 'Do you come to work by bike?'   'No, ... '
18 'Is John watching television?'   'No, ... '
19 'Does Paul swim for the school team?'   'Yes, ... '
20 'Am I sitting in the right place?'   'Yes, ... '
21 'Do you like reading poetry?'   'No, ... '
22 'Do we need our coats?'   'No, ... '
23 'Are Anne and Maria waiting for the bus?'   'Yes, ... '
24 'Are you enjoying yourself?'   'Yes, ... '
25 'Is she coming now?'   'No, ... '
26 'Does he know London well?'   'No, ... '
27 'Do they like chicken?'   'Yes, ... '

THE PAST TENSE

34 Past Simple: question and negative

FORM

- The past simple question form is the same for all persons (*I, you, he, she,* etc.) and all verbs:

Did	*Subject*	*Infinitive*
Did	I he she it we you they	leave? go? stay?

- The past simple negative form is the same for all persons and all verbs:

Subject	*did not*	*Infinitive*
I He She It We You They	did not didn't	leave. go. stay.

USE

➤ Exercise 35.

Practice

Write these sentences in the past simple, keeping them as questions or negatives.

1 Do they agree? *Did they agree?*

2 They don't drive. *They didn't drive.*

3 When do they go? ....

4 Where do they work? ....

5 Do you understand? ....

6 I don't know. ....

7 He doesn't like it. ....

8 What do you think? ....

9   She doesn't live here. ....

10 How much does it cost? ....

11 When do you get up? ....

12 I don't swim. ....

13 She doesn't speak Spanish. ....

14 We don't understand. ....

15 When do they leave? ....

16 When does he go to school? ....

17 Do you like Germany? ....

18 When do you go out? ....

19 She doesn't smoke. ....

20 He doesn't know. ....

35   Past Simple: positive – regular verbs

FORM

• Regular verbs have the same form for all persons (*I, you, he, she,* etc.):

Subject	Infinitive + *ed*
I He She It We You They	stayed.

Notes

• Irregular verbs are different in the positive ➤ Exercise 36.

• Remember to use the infinitive without *ed* for questions and negatives

➤ Exercise 34.
   Did you stay? (NOT ~~Did you stayed?~~)

• Spelling:

   a) verbs ending in *e* add only *d*:
       I love → I loved

   b) verbs ending in *y* change *y* to *ied*:
       I try → I tried

   c) most verbs ending in a single vowel + single consonant change to single
       vowel + double consonant:
       I travel → travelled
       We stop → we stopped

USE

• For a past action or state. The action can be a short one:
I **asked** *a question.*
She **missed** *the bus.*

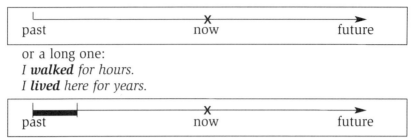

or a long one:
I **walked** *for hours.*
I **lived** *here for years.*

Practice

Change the verbs into the past simple, keeping them as positives, negatives, or questions.

1 He lives here. *He lived here.*

2 Do you work here? *Did you work here?*

3 I don't like the film. ....

4 She hates the hotel. ....

5 We don't live there. ....

6 Does he play the piano? ....

7 I love Paris. ....

8 He doesn't work very hard. ....

9 She travels a lot. ....

10 He walks everywhere. ....

11 I don't study English. ....

12 Do you drive to school? ....

13 I don't like him. ....

14 Do you miss your parents? ....

15 We love Spain. ....

16 John studies music. ....

17 Where do you live? ....

18 What does he study? ....

19 Where does she work? ....

20 We don't like London. ....

21 They hate waiting. ....

22 They work in a factory. ....

36   Past Simple: positive – irregular verbs

FORM

- Irregular verbs have the same form for all persons (*I, you, he, she,* etc)

Subject	Past Simple
I He She It We You They	went.

- Irregular verbs are irregular in the past simple in the positive only (not in the negative or question form):

  go → *went*   She **went** home yesterday.
  sit → *sat*   I **sat** down.
  write → *wrote*   She **wrote** for hours.

USE

➤ Exercise 35.

Look at these irregular forms (➤ Exercise 54 for a longer list):

go	→	went	give	→	gave
sit	→	sat	have	→	had
come	→	came	get up	→	got up
write	→	wrote	eat	→	ate
run	→	ran	drink	→	drank

Practice

Use the verbs above to complete these sentences.

1 I *wrote* a few letters yesterday.

2 He .... at six o'clock this morning.

3 They .... home late last night.

4 She .... a headache yesterday.

5 I was hungry so I .... some bread and cheese.

6 They came into my office and .... down.

7 We .... some water.

8 I was late so I .... to work.

9 She .... abroad last week.

10 They .... him some money.

37 Past Simple: positive

Practice

37a Write the past simple positive of these irregular verbs.

buy	*bought*	forget		see	
catch		give		sit	
choose		go		speak	
come		know		take	
do		make		tell	
drink		put		think	
eat		read		understand	

37b In your notebook, write these sentences putting the verbs into the past simple. Remember that the infinitive is used for questions and negatives.

1 I ...... some new clothes last week. (buy)

   I bought some new clothes last week.

2 What time ...... last night? (they come)

   What time did they come last night?

3 I ...... his question. (not understand)

   I didn't understand his question.

4 I ...... he was wrong. (think)

5 ...... a lot at the party? (you eat)

6 I ...... the bus this morning. (not catch)

7 I ...... my keys yesterday. (forget)

8 ...... you about the meeting? (they tell)

9 Peter ...... the washing up last night. (do)

10 They ...... anything at the disco. (not drink)

11 I ...... your suitcase in your bedroom. (put)

12 We ...... it was your birthday. (not know)

13 ...... to the office yesterday? (you go)

14 They ...... her a present when she left. (give)

15 We ...... their letters. (read)

38   Past Continuous

FORM

Positive				Question				Negative			
I He She It	was	working.		Was	I he she it	working?		I He She It	was not (wasn't)	working.	
We You They	were			Were	we you they			We You They	were not (weren't)		

USE

- To describe a past action at some point between its beginning and its end. The past continuous is often interrupted by the past simple.

*I **was having** a bath when the phone **rang**.*
*John **arrived** when I **was eating**.*
*I **was listening** to the radio when I **had** an idea.*
*We **were** playing tennis at 7 o'clock last night.*

Note the difference between:
a) *When she **arrived**, we **had** dinner.*
b) *When she **arrived**, we **were having** dinner.*
The time order for (a) is *arriving* then *having dinner*.
The time order for (b) is *having dinner*, during which *she arrived*.

When she arrived, we were having dinner.

Practice

38a Look at these sentences and answer the questions by circling A or B.

1   When I saw them, they were playing football.

   Which happened first?

   A I saw them   Ⓑ they were playing football

2   When she telephoned, I was having a bath.

Which happened first?

A the telephone call   B the bath

3   They were watching television when I visited them.

Which happened first?

A They were watching television   B I visited them

4   I was walking into the house when I heard the noise.

Which happened first?

A I was walking into the house   B I heard the noise

5   I walked into the house when I heard the noise.

Which happened first?

A I walked into the house   B I heard the noise.

6   We left the party when the police arrived.

Which happened first?

A We left the party   B the police arrived

7   We were leaving the party when the police arrived.

Which happened first?

A We were leaving the party   B the police arrived

8   I made the beds when Joan and Ian got here.

Which happened first?

A I made the beds   B Joan and Ian got here.

9   I was making the beds when Joan and Ian got here.

Which happened first.

A I was making the beds   B Joan and Ian got here

10 I was getting into my car when I heard the shot.

Which happened first?

A I was getting into my car   B I heard the shot

38b Complete these sentences by putting the verbs into the past continuous or the past simple.

1   I ..*was watching*.. television when the phone rang. (watch)

2   When the ambulance came, we .... him into it. (carry)

3   She .... her car when she suddenly felt ill. (drive)

4   When he saw me, he .... off the wall. (fall)

5   We .... to the radio when it suddenly stopped
    working. (listen)

6   Why .... cards when he walked into the office?
    (you play)

7   .... you when you gave them the money? (they thank)

8   .... when you turned on the gas? (you smoke)

9   When I arrived, they .... hello but continued
    working. (say)

10 When I got to the hospital, she .... in the waiting
    room. (sit)

38c In your notebook, write a question and answer in the past continuous and in
the past simple.

1 | start raining | | lie on the beach | | leave the beach |

    'What ...... you ...... it ......?'

    'We ......'

    'What were you doing when it started raining?'

    'We were lying on the beach.'

    'What did you do when it started raining?'

    'We left the beach.'

2 | arrive | | watch television | | turn off the television |

    'What ...... they ...... you ......?'

    'They ......'

    'What were they doing when you arrived?'

    'They were watching television.'

    'What did they do when you arrived?'

    'They turned off the television.'

3 | see him | | talk to Sheila | | start talking to me |

    'What ...... John ...... you ......?'

    'He ......'

4 | ring | | have a bath | | get out of the bath |

    'What ...... she ...... the phone ......?'

    'She ......'

5 | hear | | work in the office | | go straight home |

'What ...... you ...... you ...... the news?'

'I ......'

6 | start | | cook the dinner | | run out of the house |

'What ...... they ...... the fire ......?'

'They ......'

7 | fall down | | talk to a friend | | pick her up |

'What ...... she ...... the child ......?'

'She ......'

8 | start | | work in a bank | | become a soldier |

'What ...... you ...... the war ......?'

'I ......'

39   Past Simple and Past Continuous

Practice

Write **did**, **was**, or **were** to complete these sentences.

1 I .*did*. n't like it.

2 They ..*were*.. enjoying themselves.

3 .... you have a good time?

4 What time .... you leave?

5 .... he staying in a hotel?

6 I .... n't eating.

7 What .... you do then?

8 Why .... they sitting there?

9 What .... they doing?

10 What .... you say?

11 Why .... he working late last night?

12 They .... n't playing cards.

13 She .... n't understand.

14 I .... n't having a bath.

15 What .... the dog eating?

40   Past Simple and Past Continuous: short answers

'*Were you working when I phoned you last night?*' '*Yes, I was.*'
'*Did Mary ask you to work late?*' '*No, she didn't.*'

FORM

Past Simple   *Past Continuous*

Subject + ***did***		
Yes, No,	I he she it we you they	did. didn't.

Subject + ***was/were***		
Yes, No,	I he she it we you they	was. wasn't. were. weren't.

Note: The short answer to '*Did you like it?*' is '*Yes, I did.*' (NOT ~~*Yes, I liked.*~~)

Practice

Someone is asking you questions. Write the short answers.

1 'Were you sitting here yesterday?'   'No, *I wasn't.* '

2 'Did she see the accident?'   'Yes, *she did.* '

3 'Did you leave the hotel last night?'   'No, ... '

4 'Was he working when you arrived?'   'Yes, ... '

5 'Were they eating when you phoned?'   'Yes, ... '

6 'Did your father buy another car?'   'No, ... '

7 'Did you see that letter for you?'   'Yes, ... '

8 'Were your brothers sleeping when you left?'   'Yes, ... '

9 'You didn't see the accident, then?'   'No, ... '

10 'Weren't they waiting for you?'   'No, ... '

11 'Did you like the present?'   'Yes, ... '

12 'Did the children have a good time?'   'Yes, ... '

13 'Was Susan driving when you saw her?'   'No, ... '

14 'Did he speak to you?'   'Yes, ... '

15 'Did you do the washing-up?'   'Yes, ...'

16 'Were you doing your homework when I phoned?' 'Yes, ...'

17 'Was your father washing the car?'   'Yes, ...'

18 'Did you understand what he was saying?'   'No, ...'

19 'Was she leaving when you got there?'   'Yes, ...'

20 'Did your sister lose her purse yesterday?'   'Yes, ...'

41   Present Perfect

FORM

> ***has/have*** + past participle

Positive

I We You They	have ('ve)	finished.
He She It	has ('s)	

Question

Have	I we you they	finished?
Has	he she it	

Negative

I We You They	have not (haven't)	finished.
He She It	has not (hasn't)	

USE

- The present perfect describes the indefinite past:
  I've been to Paris.
  I've seen this film before.
  They've met my parents.
  The past is indefinite because the time it happened is not important, or because we do not know when it happened. Note the difference between:
  I went to Paris last year. (definite time – *past simple*)
  I've been to Paris. (at some time in my life – indefinite time – *present perfect*).

- The present perfect is often used to describe personal experience:
  I've been to Berlin.
  She's met a lot of famous people.
  I've heard this music before.

- The question form is often ***Have you ever ...?*** (= in your life?)
  Have you ever been to Paris?

- The present perfect is not used with past time words (***last night, yesterday, in 1984***, etc). It is not possible to say ~~I've seen him yesterday.~~

Note the difference between:
She's gone to Sweden. (= and she's there now)
She's been to Sweden. (= but she isn't there now)

Practice

41a Write the correct form of the present perfect to complete these sentences.

1 ..*Have you ever been*.. to Rome? (you ever be)

2 ..*I've seen*.. this film before. (I see)

3 .... in an office. (she never work)

4 .... in an aeroplane. (I never be)

5 .... to Germany? (he ever be)

6 .... my parents? (you met)

7 .... in the theatre? (you ever work)

8 .... to all the capital cities of Europe.
 (she be)

9 .... this book. (I read)

10 .... that new film about aliens? (you see)

11 .... abroad. (we never be)

12 .... a British policeman before.
 (they never see)

13 .... in a foreign country? (they ever live)

14 .... the President. (they meet)

15 .... to Brazil. (I never be)

- **'s** in a verb can be short for **is** or **has**:
 He's tired. / It's dead. / She's thirsty. (= **is**)
 He's gone. / It's disappeared. / She's left. (= **has**)

Practice

41b Are these contractions **is** or **has**?

1 He's tired. (= *is*)   6 She's worried. ....

2 She's arrived. ....   7 He's left the country. ....

3 It's escaped. ....   8 She's stopped working. ....

4 She's ill. ....   9 He's had a cold. ....

5 He's eaten. ....   10 It's died. ....

42 Present Perfect/Past Simple

Write these sentences, putting the verbs into the present perfect or past simple.

1 I (read) that book three times.

I've read that book three times.

2 She (go) home three days ago.

She went home three days ago.

3 I (meet) Mr and Mrs Shelley.

....

4 She (start) school in 1984.

....

5 I (leave) the office early last night.

....

6 He (see) the film before.

....

7 (You be) to Austria?

....

8 (You see) the film on TV last night?

....

9 When (you arrive) in London?

....

10 John (be) to Germany before.

....

11 (You read) this book before?

....

12 I (not see) him yesterday?

....

13 I never (go) anywhere by plane until now.

....

14 (You hear) their new record? It's the best they've ever made.

....

....

15 I (not know) about the disco last night.

....

43 Present Perfect + *for/since*

USE

- The present perfect + ***for/since*** is used when something started in the past and is continuing now.
  *I've worked here **for** six years.* (and I'm working here now)
  *He's lived here **since** 1990.* (and he's living here now)

NOTES

- ***for*** + period of time:
  *I've lived here **for** six years.*
  *I've worked here **for** two months.*
  *They've been married **for** a long time.*

- ***since*** + a point in time in the past:
  *I've lived here **since** 1987.*
  *I've worked here **since** February.*
  *We've been friends **since** we started college.*

- Note the difference between the present perfect and the past simple:
  *He's worked here **for** six months.* (= he's working here now)
  *He worked here **for** six months.* (= he's not working here now)

- It is not possible to say ~~He worked here since 1990.~~

Practice

43a Circle *for* or *since* in each sentence.

1 I've worked here (*for*/since) six years.

2 I lived here (*for/since*) three months.

3 I've worked in the factory (*for/since*) 1982.

4 He's been abroad (*for/since*) five years.

5 I studied French (*for/since*) twelve years.

6 I've known her (*for/since*) 1982.

7 I've lived here (*for/since*) I was a child.

8 We've been in Paris (*for/since*) we were married.

9 I've known them (*for/since*) years.

10 We practised (*for/since*) months.

43b Write these sentences, choosing ***for*** or ***since*** and putting the verb into the past simple or present perfect as necessary.

1 I (study) medicine (*for/since*) three years but then I stopped.

I studied medicine for three years but then I stopped.

2 She (work) for me (*for/since*) she left school.

She's worked for me since she left school.

3 I (work) in the restaurant (*for/since*) six months but then it closed.

....

....

4 I (live) here (*for/since*) I was a little girl.

....

5 He (be) in prison now (*for/since*) three years.

....

6 I (not see) him (*for/since*) he left the office.

....

7 I (not see) her (*for/since*) several years and then I met her again.

....

....

8 We (be) in Vienna (*for/since*) 1960.

....

9 I (work) here (*for/since*) seven years but it's time to leave now.

....

....

10 I (live) in England (*for/since*) 1993.

....

44 Present Perfect

USE

The present perfect is used to show a connection in the speaker's mind between the past and the present. This occurs in two main ways:

a) *the unfinished past*
 – by referring to something that started in the past and is continuing now:
   I've lived here for seven years. (and I live here now)
   I've worked here since 1994. (and I work here now)
➤ Exercise 43.

 – or describing something that happened in an unfinished time period:
   I've read two books this week:
   I've seen him twice today.
   She's telephoned three times this morning.

b) *the indefinite past:* referring to the past with no definite time
   (➤ Exercise 42). It is connected to the present in some way, and is often used in the following situations:

– describing something that happened in the past, when the result can be seen in the present:

He's painted his house.

Someone's taken my wallet.

She's bought a new car.

– describing something that happened recently, often when giving 'news':
Two men have escaped from prison in London.
The prime minister has arrived in Australia.
– with certain words (**just, yet, already**):
He's just gone out.
I've already told her.
Have you done your homework yet?
– describing personal experience:
I've been to Paris.
He's never been abroad.
– describing personal experience with superlatives or ordinals:
She's the most intelligent person I've met.
This is the third time we've complained.

Practice

The sentences below belong to one or more of the categories above. Complete these sentences by putting the verbs into the present perfect.

1 She *'s been* ill for several months. (be)

2 This is the nicest restaurant I .... (see)

3 Three people .... the company this week. (leave)

4 I .... three letters already. (write)

5 We .... two holidays this year. (have)

6 There .... a revolution in San Serife. (be)

7 I .... that film. (see)

8 Someone .... your front gate! (knock down)

9 It's the first time I .... (be) here.

10 .... Indonesian food? (you ever eat)

11 .... your homework yet? (you do)

12 This is the fourth time he .... my car. (damage)

13 You .... a shave! (have)

14 She's got the best voice I .... (ever hear)

15 He .... here since eight o'clock. (be)

16 The Prime Minister .... for a meeting with the President. (ask)

17 She .... (just go out)

18 I .... (never smoke)

19 This is the first time the children .... on a plane. (be)

20 .... already .... Mary? (you see)

45 Present Perfect with *just, yet,* and *already*

Notes

• Note the position of *just*, *yet*, and *already*:
just:
*He's **just** gone. / Has he **just** gone?*
yet:
*Has she gone **yet**? / Have you written that letter to Paul **yet**?*
already:
*She's **already** left. / She's left **already**. / She's left the house **already**. Has she **already** left? / Has she left **already**? / Has she left the house **already**?*

• *yet* is used only with negatives and questions:
*She hasn't phoned **yet**.*
*Has she phoned **yet**?*

Practice

In your notebook, write these sentences putting the words in brackets in the correct place. If two answers are possible, write them both.

1 I'm sorry, she's gone – she went some time ago. (already)

I'm sorry, she's already gone – she went some time ago.

I'm sorry, she's gone already – she went some time ago.

2 Have you finished? It's time to go. (yet)

3 I haven't done my homework. (yet)

4 I've told her several times that I can't come. (already)

5 You've missed her – if you hurry, you'll catch her in the street. (just)

6 Have you finished painting the house? (yet)

7 I've said that I'm not going to be here tomorrow. (already)

8 I haven't explained. (yet)

9 Have you got your passport? (already)

10 He's told me that I've got the sack. (just)

46   Present Perfect Continuous

FORM

has/have + been + verb-ing

Positive

I We You They	have ('ve)	been waiting.
He She It	has ('s)	

Question

Have	I we you they	been waiting?
Has	he she it	

Negative

I We You They	have not haven't	been waiting.
He She It	has not (hasn't)	

USE

● Frequently used with *how long, for* and *since* (➤ Exercise 43 for difference between *for* and *since*).
  I've been studying English since I was a child.
  How long *have* you *been waiting?*

● To describe activities which were happening until this moment or a very short time ago:
  'You look tired.' 'Yes, I've been working all night.'
  'Why are you so dirty?' 'I've been playing football.'

Note: this tense is not used with *to be* or with verbs that do not normally take the continuous.

Practice

Write these sentences, putting the verbs into the present perfect continuous.

1 'What (you do) today?' 'I (play) tennis.'

   'What have you been doing today?' 'I've been playing tennis.'

2 'How long (you study) English?'

   ....

3 'Oh, David! I (look) for you!'

   ....

4 'Pat (live) here for twenty-five years.

   ....

5 'I'm tired. We (walk) all day.'

   ....

6 'How long (you learn) to drive?'

   ....

7 'I (wait) here for ages.'

....

8 'She's bad-tempered because she (work) too hard.'

....

....

9 'They (watch) football since three o'clock.'

....

10 'Why (you see) your parents so much recently?'

....

....

11 'The children look exhausted. What (they do)?'

....

....

12 'She should pass the exam. She (study) for weeks.'

....

....

13 'Your mother sends her love. I (just speak) to her on the phone.'

....

....

14 'I (work) here since I was eighteen.'

....

THE FUTURE TENSE

47 Present Continuous + time word

FORM

Present continuous (➤ Exercise 29) + time word (*tomorrow, next week, on Saturday, in two weeks,* etc.):

I'm seeing them	on this } Saturday in three days in two weeks' time this week/Friday next week/Friday

USE

- To talk about plans which are arranged for a particular time in the future. This construction is used very often with **come** and **go**, and with verbs like **see, stay, visit, meet,** etc:

*They**'re going** tomorrow.*

*I**'m arriving** next week.*

*We**'re visiting** the States in three weeks.*

Notes

- Remember that a time word or expression must be used, or understood from the conversation, to make the present continuous a future.
- This is not just a 'near' future – it is possible to say: *He**'s coming back** in ten years.*

Practice

Write these sentences in full, putting the verbs into the present continuous and supply the missing words where necessary.

1 I / see / them / Saturday.

   I'm seeing them on Saturday.

2 They / come / here / three weeks.

   They're coming here in three weeks.

3 I / meet / John / three o'clock.

   ....

4 What / you do / Friday night?

   ....

5 I / go / to the disco / Saturday evening.

   ....

6 We / go back / to the States / three years.

   ....

7 They / go on holiday / two days time.

   ....

8 I / not come home / Friday.

   ....

9 You / work late / tomorrow night?

   ....

10 We / not go to school / next week.

   ....

11 He / come to see you / tomorrow.

....

12 Mr and Mrs Green / go away / three weeks.

....

13 We / have a party / Saturday.

....

14 I / see her again / next week.

....

15 You / play football / this week?

....

48 *going to*

FORM

Positive

I	am ('m)	
He She It	is ('s)	going to pay.
We You They	are ('re)	

Question

Am	I	
Is	he she it	going to pay?
Are	we you they	

Negative

I	am not ('m not)	
He She It	is not (isn't) ('s not)	going to pay.
We You They	are not (aren't) ('re not)	

USE

- To talk about a planned future action:
  *I'm **going to** see my parents on Saturday.*
  (This use is similar to *present continuous* + time word ➤ Exercise 47.)

- To talk about something in the future which we can see as a result of something happening now:
  *Look at those clouds. It's **going to** rain.*
  *That man on the bike is **going to** fall off.*

- To make statements about the future in a neutral way:
  *Alan's **going to** finish his exams on Friday.*
  *Jenny's **going to** be five next week.*
  *I'm **going to** work for a television company.*
  (The future simple is also used for the purpose ➤ Exercise 50.)

Practice

48a Write the correct form of *going to* to complete these sentences.

1 When (you) ..*are you going to*.. phone her?

2 (They not) ..*They aren't going to*... stay very long.

3 What (you) .... say to your father?

4 (I not) .... pay anything.

5 (We) .... play tennis tomorrow?

6 (She) .... live in Mexico for a few months.

7 (The machine) .... work?

8 (Your parents) .... have a holiday this year?

9 (They) .... borrow some money from the bank.

10 (I not) .... eat there again.

48b Write the correct form of *going to* and use one of these verbs to complete the sentences. Use each verb once only.

finish	complain	fall off	be	miss
die	~~rain~~	drive	work	fail

1 Look at those clouds! It *'s going to rain* .

2 Look at the sun! It .... hot today.

3 Susan's not working very hard. I think she .... her exams.

4 He's very angry. He .... to the manager.

5 It's nearly four o'clock. The lesson .... soon.

6 I don't like travelling by plane. I .... there.

7 This plan is too complicated. It (not) ....

8 The President's very ill. I think he ....

9 Watch the baby! She .... the bed!

10 This bus is very slow. I think we .... the train.

49 *going to* / Present Continuous + time word

CONTRAST

- It is often possible to use either tense:
  *I'm **seeing** them tomorrow. I'm **going to see** them tomorrow.*

- The ***going to*** future is very common, especially in conversation.
  If there is doubt about which of the two futures to use, it is better to use ***going to***.

- With the verbs ***go*** and ***come***, it is better to use the present continuous.

- Present continuous + time word is generally used for plans arranged for a particular time in the future.

Practice

In your notebook, supply the ***going to*** or present continuous future for these sentences. If two answers are possible, write them both.

1 We ...... at home tonight. (stay)

   We're going to stay at home tonight./We're staying at home tonight.

2 Look at the sky. It ...... tomorrow. (rain)

   Look at the sky. It's going to rain tomorrow.

3 We ...... at a restaurant tonight. (eat)

4 They ...... to Manchester tomorrow morning. (drive)

5 I ...... my teeth, have a wash, and go to bed. (brush)

6 Be careful with that plate! You ...... it! (break)

7 My parents ...... with us for the weekend. (stay)

8 Who's ...... him the news? (tell)

9 Hurry up! We ...... the train! (miss)

10 How many people ...... today? (arrive)

11 They ...... Nick at 10 o'clock tomorrow. (see)

12 I ...... to the seaside next weekend. (go)

13 Who ...... to John's party later? (come)

14 Bring your hat and gloves – it ...... cold later tonight. (get)

15 Mary ...... to Barbados next Tuesday. (fly)

16 Our friends ...... us before the concert. (meet)

17 We ...... into our new house next month. (move)

50 Future Simple

FORM

Positive

I He She It We You They	will ('ll)	stay.

Question

Shall/will	I	stay?
Will	he she it	
Shall/will	we	
Will	you they	

Negative

I He She It We You They	will not (won't)	stay.

Notes

- the negative contraction = **won't.**

- **shall** is not used very often now. We generally use it only as a first person question (= with **I** or **we**) to make suggestions and offers:
  Shall *I carry your suitcase for you?*
  Shall *we go to a restaurant?*

USE

- For a statement of future fact. This can be
  a) certain:
     They'll be here on Saturday afternoon.
     *The journey **will take** six hours.*
  b) uncertain:
     I think it'll rain tomorrow.
     I'm not sure he'll be there.
  Going to can also be used for this purpose ➤ Exercise 48.

- For a sudden decision to do something (usually used with **I** or **we**):
  No one's offered to help? I'll do it for you!
  Wait a minute – I'll open the door for you.
  I think I'll have eggs and chips please.

- To show willingness to do or not to do something in the future (often as a promise or a threat):
  I promise I'll be there.
  I'll never speak to him again.

He says he'll send the money.

➤ Exercise 58 for future simple in conditional sentences.

➤ Exercise 53 for future simple + **when, as soon as,** etc.

Practice

Write these sentences, putting the verbs into the future simple.

1 I'm sure he (not be) late.

I'm sure he won't be late.

2 (I open) the window for you?

Shall I open the window for you?

3 How long (the journey take?)

....

4 I suppose (she be) in London next week.

....

5 John (phone) your office for you.

....

6 (There be) a lot of people at the meeting?

....

7 What time (the race start?)

....

8 He (never agree) to your idea.

....

9 You (never see) your money again.

....

10 What's the matter? (I phone) the doctor?

....

11 Don't worry. I (pay) for the damage to your car.

....

....

12 (You be) at home tomorrow?

....

13 The company (not give) you an extra day's holiday.

....

....

14 Don't touch that! You (hurt) yourself!

....

15 There (not be) any newspapers tomorrow.

....

51 *going to* – future plan, and *will* – sudden decision

CONTRAST

- In conversation, *going to* is often used to indicate a future plan that has been made before the time of speaking:
  I'm **going to see** Pat tomorrow – *we arranged it this morning.*

- *Will* is often used to indicate a sudden decision, made at the time of speaking:
  How can we get to the airport? I know! I'**ll borrow** *Sue's car!*

Practice

Write the correct form of *going to* or *will* to complete the dialogue.

LAURA: What are you doing this weekend, Jan?

TANYA: I [1] *'m going to see* ....(see) a new play tomorrow at the
Royal Court Theatre – 'Day of the Flood'.

LAURA: Have you got the tickets yet?

TANYA: No, I [2] .... (get) them this afternoon,
actually. Would you like to come?

LAURA: Oh, thank you, that would be nice.

TANYA: OK, I [3] .... (get) you a ticket too.

LAURA: Great ... what time does it start?

TANYA: Eight o'clock, but we [4] .... (all meet) in
the Green Cafe at 7.15 ...

LAURA: OK, I [5] .... (meet) you in the cafe, but, er
... I [6] .... (be) there about half-past seven.

TANYA: That's fine.

LAURA: Oh, one other thing ... I've got no money at the moment ... I
[7] .... pay for the ticket on Saturday. Is that OK?

TANYA: Yes, that's OK, no problem.

LAURA: [8] .... (you eat) in the cafe, or just have a
cup of coffee?

TANYA: Just a coffee I think ...

LAURA: Look, [9] .... (we go) to a restaurant after the
show? I know a very good Chinese restaurant ...

TANYA: That's a good idea – I [10] .... (phone) the
others and see if they want to come too.

LAURA: Good, and then I [11] .... (book) a table ...
Great! I [12] .... (see) you tomorrow.

TANYA: Yes, see you. Bye!

52 *going to* and *will*

CONTRAST

• Sometimes it is possible to use either *going to* or *will*, but at other times only one of them is correct:

going to	1 future plan – decided before time of speaking	ex 51	I'm going to leave next week.
	2 future result from present evidence	ex 48	He's going to fall off his bike.
will	1 future willingness	ex 50	I won't do it.
	2 sudden decision made at time of speaking	ex 51	I'll phone her now.
	3 offer/suggestion	ex 50	Shall I open the door for you?
going to or *will*	1 neutral future fact[1]	ex 48 ex 56	Danny's going to be eight next week. Danny will be eight next week.
	2 first conditional[1]	ex 58	If it rains, we're going to leave. If it rains, we'll leave.
	3 *when/as soon as,* etc.[1]	ex 53	I'm going to phone when I arrive. I'll phone when I arrive.

[1]*will* is more common here.

Practice

Write the correct form of *going to*, *shall*, or *will* for these sentences. If two answers are possible, write the more likely one.

1 'Why is Sheila getting a passport?'

'She *'s going to* live in Spain for a year.'

2 'I know she ..*won't*.. (not) agree with this idea.'

3 'I think the film .... be a big success.'

4 'I don't feel very well this morning.' :

'Oh, dear. .... I look after the children for you?'

5 The managing director .... sack two hundred people next month.

6 'There's someone at the door.' 'OK, I .... answer it.'

7 She .... never see her parents again.

8 'Is that your new stereo?'

'Yes, but it doesn't work. I .... to take it back to the shop.'

9 I think the exam .... be quite easy.

10 'I see Hannah and Peter together a lot.'

'Yes. They .... get married.'

11 You .... probably have a really good time.

12 The dog looks ill. I think it .... be sick.

13 What (you) .... this weekend?

14 I .... see a late-night horror film at the Odeon.

15 You don't have to walk: I .... give you a lift.

16 I've had enough of this job. I .... leave.

17 Of course we .... help you.

53 *when* + Present Simple to describe the future

FORM

when +	*present simple*	*future simple*
When As soon as Before After If / Unless	I see him,	I'll phone you.

USE

• The present simple is used in clauses of time and condition (after **when, as soon as, if,** etc.) to refer to the future.

• **until** is similar:

future simple +	*until*	+ present simple
I'll wait	until	I see him.

Notes

• Note the use of the present simple above:
(NOT ~~When I'll see him I'll phone you.~~)
(NOT ~~I'll wait until I'll see him.~~)

• The present perfect can also be used with **when**, etc: *I'll speak to you when I've finished.*

• *Going to* or the imperative can be used, when appropriate, instead of the future simple:
*I've decided what to do. I'm **going to** talk to him when he gets here. **Phone** me when he arrives.*

Practice

Write these sentences, putting the verbs into the future simple or present simple.

1 I (give) it to them when they (visit) us.

I'll give it to them when they visit us.

2 I (not send) the parcel until I (hear) from you.

I won't send the parcel until I hear from you.

3 As soon as they (phone) me, I (contact) you.

....

4 I (see) you before I (fly) to Paris.

....

5 They (send) you the money before they (leave).

....

6 When I (talk) to him, I (give) him your news.

....

7 She (visit) her parents before she (go) to the airport.

....

....

8 I (finish) this when I (be) at the office.

....

9 I (send) you a postcard when I (get) to Bermuda.

....

....

10 She (do) her homework before she (go) out.

....

11 After I (visit) the hospital, I (go) and see her parents.

....

12 I (phone) Mary when we (get) to San Francisco.

....

13 I (call) you as soon as we (sign) the contract.

....

14 He (not do) anything before you (tell) him to.

....

15 You (be) very surprised when you (meet) him.

....

VERB FORMATIONS

54 Irregular verbs

Irregular verbs are usually listed in three different columns:

Infinitive	Past Simple	Past Participle
be	was	been
have	had	had
go	went	gone

Check

54a Add the missing words.

Infinitive	Past Simple	Past Participle	Infinitive	Past Simple	Past Participle
be	was	been			driven
beat	beat	beaten			eaten
	became			fell	
		begun	feel		
	bent			fought	
	blew				found
		broken		flew	
	brought		forget		
build			forgive		
burn				got	
	burst				given
		bought		went	
	caught		grow		
choose				heard	
come					hidden
	cost			hit	
		cut	hold		
do			hurt		
draw			keep		

Infinitive	Past Simple	Past Participle	Infinitive	Past Simple	Past Participle
dream				knew	
	drank		learn		
	left			shot	
		lent			shown
	let			shut	
lie			sing		
light			sit		
lose				slept	
	made				spoken
	meant			spent	
meet			stand		
	paid			stole	
		put			swum
	read			took	
ride			teach		
	ran		tell		
		said	think		
	saw			threw	
sell					understood
send				wore	
	set		win		
shine				wrote	

54b Complete these sentences, putting the verbs given into the past simple or present perfect.

1 They *have beaten* us at football for the last five years. (beat)

2 She *became* manager of the factory in 1982. (become)

3 We .... the meeting yesterday at 3.30 p.m. (begin)

4 The wind .... hard all through last night. (blow)

5 I'm sorry – I .... one of your glasses. (just break)

6 .... your books back already? (they bring)

7 We .... a new house last week. (buy)

8 The police .... the person who stole my purse. He's at the police station now. (catch)

9 We .... the new person for the job. (already choose)

10 Nobody .... to see me yesterday. (come)

11 It was very expensive – it .... a thousand dollars. (cost)

12 .... the washing-up yet? (you not do)

13 Someone .... into the swimming pool. (just fall)

14 I .... terrible when I woke up this morning. (feel)

15 I .... some money in the street last night. (find)

54c Complete these sentences, putting the verbs given into the present perfect or past simple.

1 .... in an aeroplane before? (you ever fly)

2 .... what I told you to do? (you already forget)

3 My parents .... me some money when I left home. (give)

4 There's nobody here – everybody .... out. (go)

5 .... when you left the dentist? (your mouth hurt)

6 I asked them to be quiet but they .... talking. (keep)

7 I .... him since we were at school together. (know)

8 I .... a lot since I started coming to this school. (learn)

9 I .... him £500. (already lend)

10 The police .... me talk to Jane after she was arrested. (let)

11 We .... the beds and cleaned the
rooms. (already make)

12 .... the taxi-driver yet? (you pay)

13 I carried the suitcases into the hall and ....
them by the front door. (put)

14 She .... most of his books
already. (read)

15 I left the house and .... quickly
down the street. (run)

54d Complete these sentences, putting the verbs given into the present perfect or
past simple.

1 I .... the doctor about it, but she couldn't help.
(already see)

2 I'm sorry, the car's not here – I .... it. (just sell)

3 She .... you a letter three weeks ago. (send)

4 I .... the door quietly when I left. (shut)

5 She .... very well, but I didn't like the band.
(sing)

6 I was so tired I .... for twelve hours. (sleep)

7 .... to John's teacher about his homework yet?
(you speak)

8 I'm afraid I .... all the money. (already spent)

9 I .... in the rain and waited for the bus. (stand)

10 .... my photograph yet? (you not take)

11 Someone .... me about your new job. (just tell)

12 She .... the ball to me and I caught it. (throw)

13 I .... what he was trying to say, but Pat didn't.
(understand)

14 She .... expensive clothes and drove a Mercedes.
(wear)

15 I .... sixty letters asking for jobs. (already write)

THE PASSIVE

55 The passive: Present Simple and Past Simple

FORM

> noun/pronoun + **to be** + past participle
> *Someone washes the car every week.*
> *The car **is washed** every week.*
>
> *They make these televisions in Japan.*
> *These televisions **are made** in Japan.*
>
> *Someone painted the house last week.*
> *The house **was painted** last week.*
>
> *They taught the children to be polite.*
> *The children **were taught** to be polite.*

USE

- The passive is used to describe actions:
  a) when we don't know who does, or did the action:
     My briefcase was stolen last night.
     (I don't know who stole it).
  b) when it is not important to know who does, or did the action:
     The cars are taken to Europe every week.
     (It doesn't matter who takes them).
     These televisions are made in Japan.
     (It doesn't matter who makes them).

My briefcase was stolen last night.

Practice

55a Rewrite these sentences in the passive.

1 Someone broke this mirror last night.

   This mirror was broken last night.

2 Someone washes the towels in the hotel every day.

   The towels in the hotel are washed every day.

3 Someone built the house ten years ago.

   ....

4 They grow this fruit in very hot countries.

   ....

5 They pay the office workers weekly.

   ....

6   Someone bought all this cheese in France.

   ....

7   Someone found Emily's bike in the river.

   ....

8   Someone visits most of the prisoners once a week.

   ....

9   Someone cleans this car every week.

   ....

10 They play a lot of sport on the beach.

   ....

11 Someone stole all my best jewellery.

   ....

12 They carried the children all the way home.

   ....

13 Someone watches the palace twenty-four hours a day.

   ....

14 They leave the grapes to dry in the sun.

   ....

55b Complete the sentences with a present passive. Use the followings verbs.

ship	pick	drink	take	dry
roast	~~prepare~~	sell	sort	~~plant~~

Growing and preparing coffee

1

The soil *is prepared.*

2

The seeds *are planted.*

3

The berries ....
by hand.

4

They ....
to a factory.

5

They .... in
the sun.

6

They .... by hand.

7

They .... all
over the world.

8

They .... in ovens
at the factory.

9

The coffee ....
in the shops.

10

It .... in offices and
homes everywhere.

55c Complete these sentences in the passive using *is*, *are*, *was* or *were* and a
word from the box.

| grown ~~cut~~ taught locked sent |
| explained ~~killed~~ given built driven |

1 His father ..*was killed*.. in the war.

2 The grass ..*is*.. never ..*cut*.. in the winter.

3 When .... these houses .... ?

4 You can't go into the school. The gates .... always ....
at 4.30.

5 .... these potatoes .... in your garden?

6 I .... a beautiful gold watch.

7 We take the bus to work during the week so the car .... only
.... at weekends.

8 The problem .... to us very clearly.

9 This letter .... never ....

10 Children .... not .... any languages at primary school
now.

55d Rewrite these sentences, putting the verbs in the passive.

1   My car / damage / last night. (past)

My car was damaged last night.

2   This computer / make / in the USA. (present)

This computer is made in the USA.

3   The machines / make / in Scotland. (present)

....

4   The President / kill / last night. (past)

....

5   The money / change into dollars / at the bank. (present)

....

....

6   The parcel / post / yesterday. (past)

....

7   Cheese / make / from milk. (present)

....

8   The children / give / some food. (past)

....

9   The house / paint / every year. (present)

....

10 Several people / hurt / in an accident last night. (past)

....

....

VERB FORMATIONS

56 *used to*

- *used to* indicates something that happened regularly in the past but doesn't happen now.
  *I **used to** smoke.* (= I don't smoke now)
  *She **used to** work for the BBC.* (= she doesn't work for the BBC now)
  *He **didn't use to** like me.* (= he likes me now)

FORM

	used to	+ *infinitive*
She	used to	live here.
I	used to	smoke.

Notes

- The negative is ***didn't use to*** + infinitive
  She didn't use to smoke.
- The question form is ***did*** + subject + ***use to*** + infinitive?
  Did you use to live here?
- The question and negative forms are not used very often.

Practice

56a Write these sentences, putting one verb into the correct form of ***used to*** and the other into the past simple.

1 I (smoke), but I (give it up) last year.

   I used to smoke, but I gave it up last year.

2 I (not like) him, but then I (change) my mind.

   I didn't use to like him, but then I changed my mind.

3 He (live) in London before he (go) abroad.

   ....

   ....

4 I (earn) a lot of money, but then I (lose) my job.

   ....

   ....

5 I'm surprised that they (join) the tennis club. They (not like) tennis.

   ....

   ....

6   (you travel) a lot before you (get) this job?

   ....

   ....

7   I (work) in a factory before I (become) a teacher.

   ....

   ....

8   She (drive) a lot before she (have) the accident.

   ....

   ....

9   That old radio (work) before I (drop) it.

   ....

   ....

10 We (see) them every week, but then we (have) an argument.

   ....

   ....

11 I (work) in a restaurant before I (go) to college.

   ....

   ....

12 She (play) a lot of tennis before she (break) her leg.

   ....

   ....

13 We (have) a garden, but then we (move) to a different house.

   ....

   ....

14 She (live) in Wales, but then she (move) back to Scotland.

   ....

   ....

15 I (drive) a lorry before I (start) this business.

   ....

   ....

- There is another construction: ***I'm used to*** + gerund: ***to be used to*** doing
   something = to be in the habit of, to be accustomed to: ***I'm used to*** *working*
   at night. (= working at night is a normal activity for me)

Note: the difference in meaning:
   I'm used to working *at night*. (= it is normal for me to do this)
   I ***used to work*** *at night*. (= I often worked at night, some time ago)

Practice

56b Circle the correct form of **used to** or **be used to**.

1   (*I'm used to* / *I used to*) live in London, but I moved.
2   (*They're used to* / *They used to*) cooking for themselves when they get home from school.
3   Do you remember how (*we used to* / *we're used to*) listen to music all the time?
4   (*Were you used to* / *Did you use to*) spend hours in front of the mirror when you were young?
5   (*I'm not used to* / *I didn't use to*) eating this sort of food.
6   (*This is used to* / *This used to*) be an industrial area.
7   (*I'm used to* / *I used to*) earn more when I was a teenager than I do now.
8   The children (*didn't use to* / *aren't used to*) going to bed so late.
9   (*I'm not used to* / *I didn't use to*) driving on the left.
10 (*I used to* / *I'm used to*) walk to work when I was younger.
11 (*I didn't use to* / *I wasn't used to*) like classical music.
12 (*I'm not used to* / *I didn't use to*) getting up so early.
13 (*I didn't use to* / *I wasn't used to*) having so much exercise.
14 (*They used to* / *They were used to*) take the children to school for us before their car broke down.
15 (*We're used to* / *We used to*) see each other every day.

57   The imperative

USE

• To give orders and instructions:
Stop!
Don't go!
Turn left at the traffic lights and then **turn right**.

FORM

• The imperative has the same form as the infinitive:
Wait!
The negative is formed by adding **don't**:
Don't wait!
Don't stop!

Notes

- The imperative is used to give instructions in the second person, i.e. *(You)* **wait**! The form is the same for the singular and the plural.

    Let's is a kind of imperative for **we**:
    Let's go.
    Let's not wait. (Note the negative.)

- The imperative is not always very polite. It is more polite to say **Could I have ...** or **Would you ...**
    Give me some bread → **Could I have** some bread, please?
    Open the door → **Would you open** the door, please?

- The imperative may sometimes be used for requests to people we know well, or for orders given by people in authority. It is often used when speaking to children or soldiers.

Practice

Mr and Mrs Brownridge are talking to their children, Joe and Emma.
In your notebook, write what they say.

1 The door's closed. Emma can open it.

2 Joe's going to touch the cooker. It's hot.

3 I don't want Emma to be late tonight.

1 Open the door, Emma!

2 Don't touch the cooker, Joe!

4 I need to lift this box. Emma can help me do it.

5 It's time for Joe to get up.

6 I want Emma to bring me another biscuit.

7 I want Joe to be quiet.

8 The window's closed: it's hot. Emma's there.

9 I'd like Emma to turn down her stereo.

10 I'd like Joe to pass the salt.

Conditionals

There are three main types of conditional. These are usually described as the first, second and third conditionals.

58 The first conditional

FORM

if + present simple	future
If you drop it,	it'll break.
If you come at ten,	we'll be ready.
If you phone me,	I'll pick you up at the park.

or future	*if* + present simple
It'll break	if you drop it.
We'll be ready	if you come at ten.
I'll pick you up later	if you phone me.

USE

• The first conditional refers to the future. It is used when there is a possibility that the *if*-event might happen.

If it rains, we'll go to the cinema. (= It might rain: it might not)
If the sun shines, we'll go to the beach. (= The sun might shine: it might not)

Note: *going to* is sometimes used in the first conditional to describe a future plan:
If it rains, we're going to visit my mother.

Practice

Write these sentences, putting the verbs in brackets into the present simple or the future simple.

1 If the train's late, we (walk).

If the train's late, we'll walk.

2 She (call) you if she (have) time.

She'll call you if she has time.

3 If it costs too much, I (buy) a smaller one.

....

4 If the doctor can't see me, I (go) somewhere else.

....

....

5   If the class (be) full, we (find) another one.

....

6   What will we do if the taxi (not come)?

....

7   Will you phone me if there (be) any problems?

....

....

8   I (ask) Peter if I (see) him tomorrow.

....

9   I (go) next week, if I (can) get a train ticket.

....

10 If I (have) to, I (complain) to the manager.

....

11 If he (see) me here, he (be) really angry.

....

12 Mary (be) worried if you don't come to the airport.

....

....

13 If it (snow) this winter, we (go) skiing.

....

14 I (lend) them some money if they (ask) me.

....

15 If you (visit) Oxford, you (see) some interesting old buildings.

....

....

59   The second conditional

FORM

if + past simple If I lived by the sea, If they asked me to work for them.	*would/could/might* + infinitive I would do a lot of swimming. I might accept.
or *would/could/might* + infinitive I would do a lot of swimming I might accept	*if* + past simple if I lived by the sea. if they asked me to work for them.

Notes

- The 'past' here is actually the subjunctive, which is the same as the past simple except for two forms – *I* and *he/she* + *were*:
  If I were you, I'd change my job.
  If John were here, he wouldn't be very happy.

- In conventional English, these two forms can be replaced by the past:
  If I was you, I'd change my job.
  If John was here, he wouldn't be very happy.

- *would* is often shortened to *'d*.

USE

- The second conditional refers to the present or future.
  The *if*-event is either
  a) hypothetical:
  If I worked in that factory, I'd soon change things. (but I don't work in that factory)
  If I spoke French, my job would be a lot easier. (but I don't speak French)

  b) unlikely:
  If she left her husband, she might be happier. (but I don't think she's going to leave her husband)

Practice

Write these sentences, putting the verbs in brackets into the correct tense.

1   If you drove more carefully, you (not have) so many accidents.

   If you drove more carefully, you wouldn't have so many accidents.

2   If he (get up) earlier, he'd get to work on time.

   If he got up earlier, he'd get to work on time.

3   If we (have) more time, I could tell you more about it.

   ....

   ....

4   If you (sell) more products, you'd earn more money.

   ....

   ....

5   I could help you if you (trust) me more.

   ....

6   His car would be a lot safer if he (buy) some new tyres.

   ....

   ....

7   The children would be better swimmers if they (go) swimming more frequently.

   ....

   ....

8   I wouldn't mind having children if we (live) in the country.

   ....

   ....

9   If I (be) you, I wouldn't worry about going to university.

   ....

   ....

10 If I (have) any money, I'd give you some.

   ....

11 Your parents (be) a lot happier if you phoned them more often.

   ....

   ....

12 Where would you like to live if you (not live) in Paris?

   ....

   ....

13 What would you do if you suddenly (win) half a million pounds?

   ....

   ....

14 Would you mind if I (not give) you the money I owe you today?

   ....

   ....

15 If I had to go to hospital, (not go) to this one.

   ....

   ....

60 First and second conditional

CONTRAST

Some students get confused by the difference between the first and second conditional. Look at these two sentences:
a) *If she works harder, she'll pass her exams.*
b) *If she worked harder, she'd pass her exams.*
The difference between the two sentences can be found by asking the question, 'Is she going to work harder?' In sentence a) the answer is, 'Maybe – and maybe not'. The answer to sentence b) is, 'Probably not'. The difference is the idea in the speaker's mind of what is going to happen. The *if*-event in a first conditional sentence is more likely to happen than the *if*-event in a second conditional.

Check

Circle the correct answer to the questions below.

1 'If Mary found out what was happening, she'd be very angry.'

Is Mary going to find out what's happening?

A Maybe   (B) Probably not

2 'If Mary finds out what's happening, she'll be very angry.'

Is Mary going to find out what's happening?

A Maybe   B Probably not

3 'If they sacked him, the factory would go on strike.'

Are they going to sack him?

A Maybe   B Probably not

4 'If they sack him, the factory will go on strike.'

Are they going to sack him?

A Maybe   B Probably not

5 'What would you do if someone told us to leave?'

Is someone going to tell us to leave?

A Maybe   B Probably not

6 'What will you do if someone tells us to leave?'

Is someone going to tell us to leave?

A Maybe   B Probably not

7 'If they don't agree with me, I'll go to the director.'

Are they going to agree with me?

A Maybe   B Probably not

8 'If they didn't agree with me, I'd go to the director.'

Do they usually agree with me?

A Maybe   B Yes   C No

9 'If I don't like your ideas, I'll say so.'

Am I going to like your ideas?

A Maybe not B Probably

10 'If I didn't like your ideas, I'd say so.'

Do I usually like your ideas?

A Maybe B Yes C No

61 Zero conditional

There is another conditional which is often called zero conditional.

FORM

if + present simple	present simple
If you press the button, If you go in the best seats,	the machine switches off. you get a free drink.
or present simple	*if* + present simple
The machine switches off You get a free drink	if you press this button. if you go in the best seats.

USE

• *If* has the same meaning as ***when*** here.

The zero conditional is used:

a) for instructions:
   If you select reverse gear, the car goes backwards.
   If the camera is on, a red light appears.

b) for general truths:
   If he's got no money, he doesn't go out.
   He always says hello if he sees you.

Practice

Put the verbs into the correct tense.

1 Water (freeze) if the temperature falls below zero.

   Water freezes if the temperature falls below zero.

2 If he's angry, his face always (go) bright red.

   ....

   ....

3 If you put your money in a savings account, you (get) ten per cent interest.

   ....

   ....

4   If the microphone isn't working, you (can not) hear what he's saying.

....

....

5   The radio (not work) if the batteries are flat.

....

6   If there (be) only a few students, we usually close one of the classes.

....

....

7   The machine (not work) if it doesn't have enough oil.

....

....

8   If a balloon is filled with hot air, it (rise).

....

9   If water (boil), it changes into steam.

....

10 The machine stops automatically if something (go) wrong.

....

....

Modals

'Modals' are the small verbs like **can**, **must**, and **might**, which give certain meanings to main verbs.

FORM

There are twelve modal verbs:

can	shall	must
could	should	ought to
may	will	need (to)
might	would	dare

- Positive is formed by putting the modal between the subject and the main verb:

  *We **should** stay.*
  *You **ought** to go.*
  *He **might** come.*

- Negative is formed by adding **not** (or **n't**) after the modal:

  *We **shouldn't** stay.*
  *You **ought not** to come.*
  *He **might not** come.*

- Questions are formed by changing the position of the modal and the subject:

  __Should__ we stay? *__Shouldn't__ we stay?*
  __Ought__ you to go? *__Oughtn't__ you to go?*
  __Might__ he come? *__Mightn't__ he come?*

Notes

- **need** can be **needn't** (modal form) or **don't need to** (verb form).
- Negative questions generally use **n't**. If **not** is used, there is a different word order:
  __Shouldn't__ we stay? *__Should__ we **not** stay?*

62   Using modals in questions and negatives

Practice

Rewrite these sentences as questions or negatives, according to the instruction given.

1   I must go to the hospital tonight. (negative)

   I mustn't go to the hospital tonight.

2   James can play the piano. (question)

   Can James play the piano?

3   Peter can pay for us. (question)

   ....

4   We must go to the passport office today. (negative)

   ....

5   We can go to the bank tomorrow. (negative question)

   ....

6   You should phone the school today. (negative)

   ....

7   You can answer all the questions. (question)

   ....

8   She can pay for the lessons. (negative)

   ....

9   You can talk to Mary for me. (question)

   ....

10 Peter can check the times of the trains for us. (question)

   ....

11 We must say goodbye to Alan and Sue. (question)

   ....

12 They can stay here for a week. (negative)

   ....

13 We can buy a return ticket here. (question)

   ....

14 They should help you. (negative)

   ....

15 He can understand me. (negative question)

   ....

63   *can, could*

- *can:* (i) *know how to, be able to:*
  *I **can** swim.*
  *Mary **can** speak French.*

  can: (ii) *be allowed to:*
  *You **can** sit here.*
  *My mother says I **can't** go out tonight.*

- *could: knew how to:*
  *Emily **could** swim when she was two.*

- **couldn't**: (i) **wasn't able to**:
  *I'm sorry, I **couldn't** come yesterday.*
  *I **couldn't** go to work this morning.*

  could/couldn't: (ii) used in the second conditional (➤ Exercise 59)
  *If you gave me the money, **could** I do the shopping?*

- Requests: both **can** and **could** are used in requests. **Could** is a little more polite:
  Can *I have a glass of water please?*
  Could *you open the door for me, please?*

Notes

- **can** refers to the future if it is followed by a time word (**next week, tomorrow,** etc):
  *I **can** do it for you next month.*

- In the negative: **can** → **can't** or **cannot**
  could → **couldn't** or **could not**.

Practice

Complete these sentences using **can** or **could**. If two answers are possible, write them both.

1   *Could*. n't you find John yesterday?

2   *Can/Could*. I come and see you tomorrow?

3   .... you pass me the salt, please?

4   .... you play the guitar?

5   Why ....'t the children go to the cinema tonight?

6   .... you help me with my suitcase, please?

7   .... you drive my car if you had to?

8   .... you answer the phone for me?

9   Why ....'t you come to the disco tomorrow?

10 It was very difficult to hear: I ....n't understand what she was saying.

11 .... I smoke in here?

12 We had an appointment yesterday afternoon, but he ....n't see me.

13 I .... do the job for you next year.

14 .... you tell me the time, please?

15 I ....n't find my front door key last night.

64   *may, might*

- *may* and *might* indicate present or future possibility:
  *He **might** arrive soon.*
  *He **may** arrive soon.*
  *She **might** be angry if you do that.*
  *She **may** be angry if you do that.*

- ***May** I?* or ***May** we?* are used for polite requests, in the same way as ***Can** I?* or
  ***Can** we?* (➤ Exercise 63). It is a very polite form:
  ***May** I ask you a question?*
  ***May** I have a glass of water, please?*

May I ask you a question?

Notes

- *may* is occasionally used in formal English to mean ***to be allowed to***:
  *Guests **may** bring husbands or wives if they wish.*

- *may* and *might* are usually used in question form only with *I* or *we*: other persons more
  often use the positive with ***Do you think** …?*:
  *He **might** be late.* ➝ *Do you think he **might** be late?*

- The negative of *may* is *may not*. (NOT ~~mayn't~~).
  The negative of *might* is *might not* or *mightn't*.

Practice

64a Rewrite these sentences using *may* or *might*. Where two answers are
possible, write them both.

1   Maybe he'll get a new job.

   He might/may get a new job.

2   Do you think I could have one of these cakes?

   May I have one of these cakes?

3   Maybe there's some tea in the pot.

   ....

4   Would you mind if I asked you how old you are?

   ....

5   Visitors are not allowed to stay in the hospital after ten p.m.

   ....

   ....

6   Do you think I could have one of these sandwiches?

   ....

7   I think the car is in the station car park.

   ....

8 Is it all right if I use your phone?

....

9 Guests are allowed to wear casual dress.

....

10 Maybe she'll move to London.

....

11 There's a possibility that the show will be cancelled.

....

12 Maybe she'll be elected.

....

13 I think that Andrew will collect the money.

....

14 Maybe Peter won't come to the cinema tomorrow.

....

....

15 Maybe it'll rain this afternoon.

....

64b Complete the telephone conversation using *may* (*not*) or *might* (*not*). Where two answers are possible, write them both.

RECEPTIONIST: Good morning, Bentley Supplies, how [1]....................... I help you?

CALLER: [2]....................... I speak to John Brown, please?

RECEPTIONIST: I'm afraid he isn't here this morning. Can I take a message?

CALLER: No, I need to speak to him personally. Do you know what time he [3]....................... be back?

RECEPTIONIST: He [4]....................... be back for an hour after lunch but he [5]....................... make it if the traffic is bad.

CALLER: I [6]....................... be able to call this afternoon as I have a meeting. Could you tell John that I'll phone him this evening at home?

RECEPTIONIST: Certainly. [7]....................... I have your name please?

CALLER: Yes, it's David Marks.

65 *can, could, may, might, should, must*

- ***must/mustn't*** is stronger that ***should/shouldn't***:
  *You **must** take your passport when you travel abroad.* (obligation)
  *I think it's going to rain. You **should** take an umbrella.* (advice)

Check

65a Write the sentences, choosing one of the modals.

1 We are leaving tonight, so you (*should/must*) buy a ticket for the flight.
   We are leaving tonight, so you must buy a ticket for the flight.

2 (*May/Might*) I come in?

   ....

3 David (*can/could*) cook well when he wants to.

   ....

4 'Do you think it (*can/might*) rain?'

   ....

   'Yes, possibly. We don't want to get wet so I think we (*should/must*) take
   our raincoats.'

   ....

   ....

5 Jenny tried to carry him but she (*can't/couldn't*).

   ....

6 We (*can/might*) visit my cousin in Australia next year but we don't
   know yet.

   ....

   ....

7   In many countries, you (*should/must*) wear a seat belt in the car – it's
   the law.

   ....

   ....

8 (*Can/May*) you hold this for me, please?

   ....

9 I know they enjoy their work but they (*shouldn't/mustn't*) work at the
   weekends. It's not good for them. I think they (*should/must*) spend time
   at home with their families.

   ....

....

....

10 The letter (*can/may*) arrive tomorrow.

....

65b Complete the sentences with **can, could, may, might, should** or **must** in the positive or negative.

1 Richard's only three but he *can* swim very well.

2 You've had that headache for two days. I think you .... go to the doctor.

3 I don't think we .... go to the beach because it .... rain this afternoon.

4 I lived in Germany as a child so I .... speak German then but I .... speak it now.

5 You .... remember to take your passport tomorrow.

6 .... you close the door, please?

7 We .... move house next year but we're not sure yet.

8 Passengers .... smoke when the plane is taking off.

9 I think you .... play tennis with Sally – she .... play really well.

10 'Do you think I .... learn some Portuguese before I go to Brazil?' 'Yes, that would be a good idea.'

11 We .... remember to pay this bill before the weekend – it's very important. If we don't, we'll have no electricity.

12 I know you like sugar but you .... eat quite so much – it's bad for you.

13 I'll be at work on Saturday so I'm afraid I .... come to the football match with you.

14 I was listening very carefully but I .... hear what she said.

15 They don't like living in the countryside – it's too quiet. I think they .... move back to the city but they don't agree.

66   *I have to be there at 9 o'clock: have + to-*infinitive

FORM

Present

I You We They	have to	do it.
She He It	has to	

Past

I You We They She He It	had to	do it.

- The verb **have** + the **to-**infinitive.

Note: **have** + **to-**infinitive has its own meaning and in this way it is like a modal verb. However, it does not have the form of a modal – it is an ordinary verb and we can use it in any tense. The form of the positive, negative and question is the same as for other verbs.

USE

- **have** + **to-**infinitive = It is very important to do something/It is necessary to do something.

- **not have** + **to-**infinitive = It is not necessary to do something.

- **have** + **to-**infinitive is very similar in meaning to **must** but we can use it for all tenses. We can say:
  We **must** leave early. or
  We **have to** leave early. but only
  We **had to** leave early last night. (We do not use **must** in the past.)

- **must** and **have** + **to-**infinitive have different meanings in the negative:
  You **mustn't** stay here. It's very dangerous.
  (= It is very important that you don't stay here.)
  You **don't have to** wait for me. I can get a taxi home. ·
  (= It is not necessary for you to wait for me, but you can wait if you want to.)

Practice

66a Complete the sentences with **have** + **to-**infinitive in the correct form and one of the verbs below. Use **have** in the present simple.

read	explain	shout	~~be~~	stop
come	~~get up~~	sleep	talk	end
open	answer	decide	take	turn

1   I ...*have to be*... at work at 9 o'clock in the morning. (positive)

2   We ...*don't have to get up*... early at weekends. (negative)

3   She .... all the phone calls at work. (positive)

4 .... you .... all these books for the exam? (question)

5 I .... which job I want before the end of the week. (positive)

6 You .... – I can hear you. (negative)

7 .... the hotel staff .... in the hotel? (question)

8 We .... the bus into town. We can walk. (negative)

9 She .... the shop at 9 o'clock every morning. (positive)

10 You .... quietly in the library. (positive)

11 .... I .... right at the traffic lights to get to the hospital? (question)

12 You .... it to me. I understand the problem. (negative)

13 We .... talking when the lesson starts. (positive)

14 '................................ your little sister .... to town with us?' 'Yes, she does. I'm looking after her today.' (question)

15 You .... the present by post. I will see him tomorrow and I can give it to him then. (negative)

66b Rewrite the sentences adding *have* + *to*-infinitive in the correct tense and form.

1 Did you take a taxi home?

Did you have to take a taxi home?

2 I've used the bus for the last two days.

I've had to use the bus for the last two days.

3 I do the washing once a week.

....

4 We didn't go to college yesterday.

....

5 Did you get up early this morning?

....

6 I'll start work next week.

....

7 I've always worked hard.

....

8   The children go to bed at 8 o'clock.

....

9   They don't work on Saturdays.

....

10 Did you take your lunch with you?

....

11 She worked very hard for her exam.

....

12 I usually cut the grass once a week.

....

13 She didn't cook the dinner last night.

....

14 Do you pay to go in?

....

15 I usually stay at home on Wednesdays.

....

66c Complete the sentences with *mustn't* or the correct form of *not have to*.

1   You ..*mustn't*.. smoke at petrol stations.

2   She ..*doesn't have to*.. come if she doesn't want to.

3   We .... miss the train. It's the last one tonight.

4   I .... do this work tonight. I can do it tomorrow.

5   I .... clean the floor today. I cleaned it yesterday.

6   We .... forget to lock all the doors before we go away.

7   They .... sit in the sun for too long. They might get burnt.

8   We .... stay in a hotel in London. We can stay with my cousin.

9   He .... come home too late. He's got an important day tomorrow.

10 We .... spend too much money tonight. We've only got a little left.

Gerunds and infinitives

THE GERUND

67 The gerund

- The gerund is used like a noun:
  Smoking *is bad for you.*
  Do you like **watching** *TV?*
  She's good at **swimming**.

- It is formed by adding **ing** to the infinitive:
  go → *go***ing**
  stay → *stay***ing**
  The negative is formed by adding **not**:
  Would you mind **not smoking**?

Note: the changes that are sometimes necessary:
lie → *lying* (**ie** → **y**)
take → *taking* (single *e*: *e* is omitted)
sit → *sitting* (single vowel + single consonant → single vowel + double consonant)

Practice

67a In your notebook, write the gerund of these verbs.

do	swim	fly
play	run	try
travel	lie	get
ride		

67b Fill the gaps with gerunds from the above box. Use each verb once only.

1 She likes ..*running*.. every morning before breakfast.

2 After .... my homework, I usually watch TV.

3 I enjoy .... on the beach.

4 She doesn't like .... with other children.

5 .... is a fast way of ....

6 She likes sport, especially .... horses and ....

7 After .... several times, I finally passed my exams.

8 I lay in bed and thought about .... up.

68 *like, dislike* and other verbs + gerund

- Some verbs can be followed by a gerund or a noun, including the following:

like	love	finish	start
dislike	hate	stop	enjoy
prefer	miss	give up	begin

Note: *like, love, prefer,* and *start* are sometimes followed by the infinitive.

Practice

Write these sentences, changing the verbs into gerunds.

1   Do you like (make) cakes?

 Do you like making cakes?

2   I dislike (get up) at seven o'clock every morning.

 ....

3   I started (work) here eight or nine years ago.

 ....

4   Do you prefer (travel) by plane or by ship?

 ....

5   I hate (write) 'thank you' letters.

 ....

6   I gave up (drive) after I had a bad accident.

 ....

7   I miss (be) able to visit my family.

 ....

8   I love (sit) here by the sea in the evenings.

 ....

9   I think it's time to stop (play) football.

 ....

10 What time did you finish (read) last night?

 ....

11 Why don't you like (go) to discos?

 ....

12 I think I'll start (pack) my suitcase.

 ....

69   Prepositions + gerund

- When a verb follows an preposition, it takes the gerund:
  *We thought **about leaving** early.*
  *I was worried **about getting** home.*
  *I'm interested **in hearing** more about your offer.*
  *I'm tired **of hearing** his excuses.*
  ***After closing** the door, he looked up and down the street.*
  *Check your passport **before leaving**.*

NOTES

- Note that *to* can be a preposition, or part of an infinitive:
  *I decided **to leave** early. (**to** + infinitive)*
  *I'm looking forward **to seeing** them again. (**to** + gerund)*

- A gerund behaves like a noun. Where a gerund can be used, a noun can also be used.
  *I'm looking forward to **going** on holiday.*
  I'm looking forward to my holiday.

Practice

Complete these sentences, putting the verbs into the gerund and using one of the following prepositions. Some of them are used more than once.

about	of	in	to	after
by	for	on	at	without

1   We talked ..*about going*.. (go) to France for our holiday.

2   I look forward .... (see) you again next year.

3   She's tired .... (work) for the company.

4   I'm very happy .... my parents

    .... (come) home.

5   .... (open) the front door, I walked slowly through it.

6   We got into the house .... (climb) through
    a window.

7   I'm looking forward .... (work) with you.

8   Are you interested .... (join) the committee?

9   I'm tired .... (come) to the same place every week.

10 He's very keen .... (swim) at the moment.

11 I'm worried .... Jane ....(get)
    to the airport on time.

12 I'm not interested .... (hear) your excuses.

13 She's very good .... (listen) to what people say.

14 This is used .... (cut) metal.

15 The car drove off .... (stop).

70 Gerunds as subjects of sentences

- Gerunds can be subjects of sentences (or objects ➤ Exercise 67):
Smoking makes me feel sick.
Living in a foreign country can be very difficult.

Practice

Rewrite these sentences, starting with a gerund. You may need to change some words.

1 A good way of keeping fit is to swim every day.

Swimming every day is a good way of keeping fit.

2 It takes a long time to learn a foreign language.

....

....

3 Clean the machine more often – that will solve your problems.

....

4 Grow your own food. It's less expensive.

....

5 Give up smoking: it will make you feel better.

....

6 It is cheaper to go by rail than by air.

....

7 You are not allowed to smoke here.

....

8 It's not very pleasant to be in hospital.

....

9 It's very difficult to windsurf properly.

....

10 It's more difficult to speak a foreign language than to read it.

....

11 It is forbidden to walk on the grass.

....

12 One thing I can't do is swim on my back.

....

13 It's difficult to be polite to someone you don't like.

....

71 Gerunds

Check

have	study	~~smoke~~	work	live
move	get up	say	go	make
watch	help	eat	write	see
learn	look after	become	walk	go out

Write the verbs in the box in the correct form in these sentences. Use each verb once only.

1 ..*Smoking*.. is unhealthy, but a lot of people find it difficult to stop.

2 I'm fed up with .... in the city – it's too dirty and crowded.

3 I enjoy .... in the garden at weekends.

4 I have decided to stop .... in the evenings so that I can save some money for my holidays.

5 He's an artistic person – very good at .... poetry.

6 They don't like .... and go everywhere by car.

7 I'm not really interested in .... to university.

8 She's going to continue .... for another two years, until her exams.

9 They're thinking of .... house.

10 That machine? Oh, it's used for .... toasted sandwiches.

11 They've given up .... meat.

12 Before .... a teacher, he worked in advertising.

13 .... children can be very tiring.

14 We're looking forward to .... you.

15 They hate .... early in the morning.

16 Thank you for .... me organize the party.

17 They're very keen on .... how to play chess.

18 We love .... parties.

19 She left without .... goodbye.

20 .... television seems to be our national sport.

THE INFINITIVE

FORM

- Depending on the construction, infinitives are used with or without **to**:

*It's time **to go**.*
*Did you see the accident **happen**?*

72   *to* + infinitive after certain verbs

- Certain verbs take the infinitive.

*I want **to stay**.*
*We decided **to wait** for the bus.*

Note the negative:
  *We decided **not to wait** for the bus.*

Practice

Complete the sentences, using a verb from the box. Use each verb once.

help	stay	find
speak	look after	telephone
buy	~~go~~	go out
get on		

1   We decided .*to go*. to Spain for our holidays.

2   She learnt .... Arabic when she was a child.

3   I tried .... you but there was no answer.

4   They refused .... the plane.

5   She hopes .... a job soon.

6   Did you forget .... the bread?

7   I'm tired: I don't want .... tonight.

8   They offered .... the children for the evening.

9   They're planning .... with us for the weekend.

10 He agreed .... us with our problem.

73   *to* + infinitive to express purpose

- *to* + infinitive is used to express purpose:

*I came here **to see** you.*
*I went to London **to study** English.*
*I drove to the airport **to meet** my parents.*

Practice

Express each question and answer as one sentence, using *to* + infinitive. Note that you will need to change some words.

1   Q: Why do you go to the beach every weekend?

   A: Because I like swimming.

   She goes to the beach every weekend to swim.

2   Q: Why did you move to London?

   A: I wanted to find work.

   He ....

3   Q: Why are you leaving home?

   A: I'm going to university in Birmingham.

   She ....

   ....

4   Q: Why are you having a party?

   A: It's my thirtieth birthday, and I want to celebrate it.

   He ....

   ....

5   Q: Why do you get up at six every morning?

   A: I do my training then.

   She ....

   ....

6   Q: Why are you going out?

   A: I want to post a card to my mother.

   He ....

7   Q: Why are you saving money?

   A: We want to buy a car.

   They ....

8   Q: Why are you going to Egypt?

A: We want to visit Ali's parents.

They ....

9   Q: Why did you buy a new suit?

A: I want to wear it at the office party.

He ....

....

10 Q: Why did you buy a video recorder?

A: We want to record the World Cup Final.

They ....

....

74   *in order to* + infinitive, *so as to* + infinitive to express purpose

In order to + infinitive and *so as to* + infinitive are also used to express purpose.

* *in order to* + infinitive, can be more formal than *to* + infinitive:
  In order to qualify for the award, you should be under twenty-five.

* *in order to* + infinitive and *so as to* + infinitive are more common than *to* + infinitive before verbs like *be, have,* and *know*:
  I got up early so as to be ready for John's phone call.

* To express a negative purpose, *in order not to* + infinitive and *so as not to* + infinitive are more common than *not to* + infinitive:
  He opened the door quietly so as not to disturb the baby.

Practice

Rewrite these sentences without changing their meaning, using the words in brackets. You will need to omit some words, and you may need to change the word order.

1   She put the letter in her bag because she didn't want to lose it. (so as)
    She put the letter in her bag so as not to lose it.

2   You should book your tickets early if you want to avoid disappointment.
    (in order to)
    You should book your tickets early in order to avoid disappointment.

3   I'll leave work at 4.30 so I won't be late. (so as)
    ....

4   Everybody stopped talking because they wanted to hear her sing.

(in order)

....

....

5   I need to watch you so I can understand what you are doing on the computer. (in order)

....

....

6   If you want to pass the exam, you will need to study very hard. (in order)

....

....

7   We don't want to waste any time, so let's start the meeting now. (so as)

....

....

8   They moved out of the city because they wanted to have a quieter life. (in order)

....

....

9   Keep the CD in its case. Then you won't damage it. (so as)

....

....

10 He waited outside the house because he wanted to see her when she came home. (so as)

....

....

Reported speech

There are two ways of reporting what a person says:

- *Direct speech*
  He said, 'I'm going home.'
  'I'm going home,' he said.

- *Indirect speech*
  He says he's going home.
  He said he was going home.

DIRECT SPEECH

75 Writing direct speech

She said, 'My name's Stella.'
'My name's Stella,' she said.

- Direct speech report the exact words the speaker says. Put quotation marks ('...') before and after the speaker's statement.

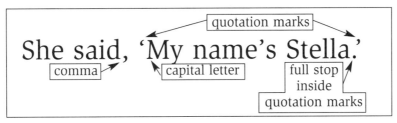

Notes

- The speaker's statement always starts with a capital letter.

- *she said* can go before or after the statement, but is separated from it by a comma (,).
  Commas and full stops after the statement go inside the quotation marks.
  Question marks go inside the quotation marks.
  Question marks are not followed by a comma:
  'How are you?' she said.

Practice

75a Put the sentences below into direct speech, using the words given.

1   the bus driver

The bus driver said, 'We're late.'

2   the little boy

....

3   Jane

....

4   the policeman

....

5   the old man

....

....

6 the teacher

....

....

7 she

....

....

8 he

....

....

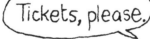

9 the guard

....

10 the receptionist

....

....

75b Write the sentences below using direct speech. Write each sentence twice, putting *she said, he said,* etc. before and after the statement.

1 *Don't be late home.*

My parents *said, 'Don't be late home.'*
'Don't be late home,' my parents said.

2 *I'd like to go out tonight.*

He *said, 'I'd like to go out tonight.'*
'I'd like to go out tonight,' he said.

3 *Read this book before next week.*

The teacher ....
....

4 *Go home and stay in bed.*

The doctor ....
....

5 *We're coming to visit you on Sunday.*

Ruth ....
....

6 *The courses cost £100 per week.*

The receptionist ....
....

7 *We had a lovely time.*

They ....
....

8 *I want to come with you.*

Danny ....
....

9 You're on the
   wrong train.   The ticket inspector ....

   ....

10 Can you answer
    the door?   My grandmother ....

    ....

76   *say, tell*

CONTRAST

- *tell* has a personal direct object (e.g. *me, him, her,* etc. ➤ Exercise 79)

  *She **told me** she was going to be late.*
  *'It's too late,' she **told me**.*
  (We cannot say: ~~He told the weather was nice.~~)

- *tell* is not used before questions. (We cannot say: ~~He told me, 'Have we met before?'~~)

- *say* never has a personal direct object:

  *She **said** she was going to be late.*
  *'It's too late,' she **said**.*

  The indirect object (**to me, to her, to us,** etc. ➤ Exercise 79) is used instead.

  *'I don't like them very much,' she **said to me** quietly.*
  *Why did **he say** that **to you**?*

- There are a few special phrases in which *tell* does not have to take a personal direct object:

tell the truth	*tell the time*
tell a lie	*tell a story*
tell lies	

Practice

76a Use the correct form of *say* or *tell* in these sentences.

1 She ..*told*.. me she didn't agree.

2 'I think I've met you before,' he ..*said*..

3 I .... them I wasn't happy with their work.

4 She .... me a story about her parents.

5 He ...., 'Are you feeling OK?'

6 She smiled, and .... to me, 'I'm very pleased to meet you.'

7   I didn't hear: what did she ....?

8   Could you .... me the time, please?

9   They .... me they were going to a meeting.

10 I .... the policeman my address.

11 I .... I wanted to buy a magazine.

12 He .... he wasn't interested in politics.

13 Could you .... me your name again, please?

14 Do you think he's .... the truth?

15 Would you .... them to come early tomorrow?

16 If he .... that again, there'll be trouble.

17 I .... them it was dangerous to swim there.

18 Did you .... anything to him about your problems at work?

19 .... me what happened.

20 I think he's .... lies.

76b Circle the correct verb, *say* or *tell*, in each sentence.

1   They (*say/tell*) that they're going to London to see Frank.

2   Mark (*said/told*) us all about his holiday in Jamaica.

3   Did you (*say/tell*) Sally is coming with us?

4   The teacher (*said/told*) the class a funny story.

5   'Don't (*say/tell*) lies!' (*said/told*) James angrily.

6   How old were you when you learned to (*say/tell*) the time?

7   I can't understand what they're (*saying/telling*) to each other.

8   I hate speaking in public. I never know what to (*say/tell*).

9   Jane always (*says/tells*) me her secrets.

10 'Do you think anyone saw us?' she (*said/told*) nervously.

INDIRECT SPEECH

77 Reported statements with no change of tense

- When the reporting verb is present, present perfect, or future, there is no change of tense in the reported statement:

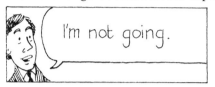

I'm not going.

= He says **he isn't** going.
= He'll say **he isn't** going.
= He's said **he isn't** going.

Note: **that** can be used after the main verb. The use of **that** is optional:
He says **that** he isn't going.
He says he isn't going.

Practice

Write these sentences in indirect speech, using the words given. Remember to change the pronouns where necessary.

1 'I haven't done my homework.' (she says)

She says she hasn't done her homework.

2 'I haven't got any money.' (He'll tell you)

He'll tell you he hasn't got any money.

3 'I've seen the film before.' (she says)

....

4 'I want to go home.' (he's already told you)

....

5 'I haven't seen my mother for years.' (he says)

....

6 'I don't know how much it costs.' (she says)

....

7 'I don't like going to parties.' (she's told me)

....

8 'We've never been to Berlin.' (they say)

....

9 'I need the money to visit my parents.' (he'll say)

....

....

10 'We can't come on Tuesday.' (they've told me)

....

....

11 'I'm going to visit Europe this year.' (the President will announce that)

....

....

12 'I can't stand classical music.' (Gemma tells me)

....

....

13 'The plane will land in half and hour.' (the pilot has just announced that)

....

....

14 'There are no tickets left for tonight's performance.' (the booking office says that)

....

....

15 'We haven't had anything to eat.' (the children say)

....

....

16 'I've already seen the play.' (he's told me)

....

17 'I'll come again next year.' (I've told them)

....

18 'I'm not feeling very well.' (Simon says)

....

19 'I've never been to Japan.' (Jason has just said)

....

....

20 'I'm meeting the students for lunch next week.' (she'll tell you)

....

....

21 'You'll never drive a better car.' (the advertisement claims that)

....

....

78   Reported statements with a change of tense

- When the main verb of the sentence is in the past tense, the tense in the reported statement is changed:

= He said he **wasn't** going.
He said that he **wasn't** going.

= She said her name **was** Stella.
She said that her name **was** Stella.

FORM

Speaker's words		Reported statement
present simple	→	past simple
present continuous	→	past continuous

Practice

Write these sentences in indirect speech, using the words given. Change the pronouns where necessary.

1 'My name's Ian.' (he said)

   He said his name was Ian.

2 'I'm writing a letter.' (she said)

   She said she was writing a letter.

3 'I'm waiting for Jessie.' (she said)

   ....

4 'I don't like the idea.' (he said)

   ....

5 'The car isn't at my house.' (she said)

   ....

6 'The washing machine's broken.' (he said)

   ....

7 'I'm working.' (he said)

   ....

8 'We're worried about Peter.' (they said)

   ....

9 'I don't smoke.' (Megan said)

....

10 'I'm waiting for my exam results.' (John said)

....

11 'I work for an American company.' (Mrs Johnson said)

....

....

12 'I feel ill.' (the little boy said)

....

13 'I'm watching television.' (Fiona said)

....

14 'I like the new house.' (Sam said)

....

15 'I'm washing the car.' (Chloe said)

....

Sentence structure

WORD ORDER

79   Direct object and indirect object

- In simple sentences the object is easy to see:
  *She hit **him**.*
  *They took **the money**.*

- Some verbs, however, have two objects:
  *She gave **me the book**.* (= she gave the book to me)
  the book is the real object of this sentence. It tells us **what** she gave.
  This is the direct object (D.O.)
  me is the indirect object (I.O.)

FORM

- verb + direct object + **to** or **for** + indirect object:

	D.O.		I.O.
Give	the money	to	him.
Buy	a present	for	your mother.

   a) Some common verbs taking **to: bring, give, lend, pay, promise, send, show, take, tell.**

   b) Some common verbs taking **for: buy, find, get, make.**

- verb + indirect object without **to** or **for** + direct object:

	I.O.	D.O.
Give	him	the money.
Buy	your mother	a present.

Note: that it is not possible to use the second form when the direct object is a pronoun (***me, her, him, it,*** etc). The longer construction must be used:
Give it to John. (NOT ~~Give John it.~~)

Practice

79a Rewrite these sentences without using **to** or **for**.

1   Give this food to your parents.

   Give your parents this food.

2   Get an ashtray for me, please.

   Get me an ashtray, please.

3   Have you sent a postcard to your family?

   ....

4   Did you pay the money to him?

   ....

5   Would you find a seat for my mother, please?

....

6   I'll get some money for you.

....

7   Did you tell the news to your parents?

....

8   I'm buying a ticket for Jenny, too.

....

9   Show your painting to Mr Anderson.

....

10 Would you take this note to your parents?

....

79b Rewrite these sentences in the correct order.

1   to my parents / I / it / took
    I took it to my parents.

2   they / any money / me / didn't give
    They didn't give me any money.

3   to all / she / the car / her friends / showed

....

4   the students / the news / gave / I

....

5   did / my pen / lend / you / him?

....

6   bought / some flowers / my / I / parents / for

....

7   why / some perfume / didn't / me / bring / you?

....

8   some grapes and some flowers / took / Janice / we

....

9   his / showed / injured / me / hand / he

....

10 some vegetables from the garden / gave / our neighbours / we / to

....

....

80 Frequency adverbs with the Present Simple

FORM

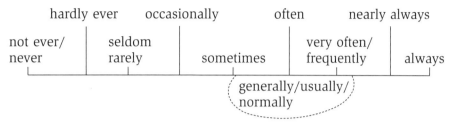

USE

- The adverb goes between the subject and the verb:
  *I **often** see them.*
  *We **rarely** talk to them.*
  *I **seldom** go out in the evenings.*

- ***occasionally, sometimes, often, frequently,*** and ***normally*** can also be at the beginning or end of a clause:
  *I see them **occasionally**.*
  ***Sometimes** we talk to each other.*
  ***Normally** I go out in the evenings.*

Note: ***always*** is sometimes used with present continuous to express annoyance. ***always*** goes between the auxiliary verb and the main verb:
*Sams's **always** borrowing my things without asking!*
*Peter's **always** complaining about his job!*

Practice

Do this exercise in your notebook. Choose the correct word and write it in its proper place in these sentences.

1 I see them nowadays – the last time we met was ten years ago.

(never / often / always)

I never see them nowadays – the last time we met was ten years ago.

2 You're lucky: we have ice cream, but we've got some today.

(hardly ever / normally / nearly always)

3 Peter's playing football instead of doing his homework.

(seldom / hardly ever / always)

4 We go out now – we can't afford it. (hardly ever / sometimes / frequently)

5 I don't finish work before eleven o'clock, so I see the children before they go to bed. (always / never / usually)

6 I sit here when I come to the park – it's my favourite place.

(hardly ever / occasionally / always)

7 She comes here nowadays – I don't think she likes me.

(seldom / frequently / nearly always)

8 We don't go there every week, but we see them quite.

(seldom / often / occasionally)

9 We see them, at least once a week. (frequently / occasionally / always)

10 I watch horror movies – I don't like them. (frequently / nearly always / hardly ever)

81   Link words: *and, but, so, then, before, after, because*

Practice

Write one of the above words in the correct place in these sentences. Use each word for two sentences. Where two answers are possible, choose the more likely one.

1 I got out of the car ..*and*.. walked into the house.

2 The weather was lovely .... we stayed in the garden.

3 .... we went to bed, I locked all the doors.

4 The little boy was wet and cold .... he wasn't hurt.

5 We turned off the lights and .... left the room.

6 I had a bath .... we played football.

7 I sat in the kitchen .... read a book.

8 She worked hard .... failed all her exams.

9 I do some exercises .... I go to work in the morning.

10 They took me to hospital .... the crash.

11 We had no money .... the banks were closed.

12 We paid our hotel bill and .... left.

13 I had to walk to work .... the car wouldn't start.

14 It was very cold .... we didn't go out.

82 Link words: *because, as, since*

Practice

Link the two sentences to make one sentence, using the word given. Don't change the order of the two original sentences. Use a comma if the link word comes at the beginning of your sentence.

1 She was very tired. She went to bed. (as)

As she was very tired, she went to bed.

2 I can't use my car. It's broken down. (because)

I can't use my car because it's broken down.

3 He hasn't done any work. I don't think he'll pass the exam. (since)

....

....

4 The bus crashed. The driver fell asleep. (because)

....

5 It was raining. We decided not to go out. (as)

....

6 The climate is changing. The earth is getting warmer. (because)

....

7 Monday is a public holiday. We're going to spend the weekend in the mountains. (since)

....

....

8 Romeo committed suicide. He thought Juliet was dead. (because)

....

....

9 You haven't seen the cathedral yet. I'll take you there on Sunday. (as)

....

....

10 The concert was cancelled. The singer was ill. (because)

....

....

83   *both ... and, neither ... nor*

- *Maria comes from Colombia. Felipe also comes from Colombia.*
  *Maria **and** Felipe **both** come from Colombia. **Both** Maria **and** Felipe come from Colombia.*

- *The police couldn't catch him. The army couldn't catch him. **Neither** the police **nor** the army could catch him.*

Practice

Rewrite the two sentences as one sentence using ***both ... and*** or ***neither ... nor***.

1   Greg likes surfing. Liz likes surfing.

   Both Greg and Liz like surfing. Or: *Greg and Liz both like surfing.*

2   The house wasn't attractive. The garden wasn't attractive.

   Neither the house nor the garden were attractive.

3   The food was terrible. The service was terrible too.

   ....

4   Angela played the piano. Lucy also played the piano.

   ....

5   Jessica wasn't at home. Chloe wasn't at home.

   ....

6   His family didn't know about his accident. His friends didn't know about his accident.

   ....

   ....

7   Eagles hunt small animals. Wolves hunt small animals.

   ....

8   The film is very funny. The book is also very funny.

   ....

9   The beach isn't far away. The shops aren't far away.

   ....

10 Japan has a lot of earthquakes. California has a lot of earthquakes.

   ....

QUESTIONS AND ANSWERS

84   Making questions

- Questions are formed for all tenses except present simple and past simple by changing the position of the auxiliary verb (**am, was, will,** etc.) and the subject (**I, you, she, he,** etc.):

  You're going → **Are you** going?

  He has gone → **Has he** gone?

- Questions are formed for the present simple and past simple by using **do, does,** or **did**:
  They work here. Do they work here?
  She lived here. Did she live here?

➤ Exercise 28 and 34 for present simple and past simple.

Practice

84a Make questions from these statements.

1   She likes travelling

   Does she like travelling?

2   They're working.

   Are they working?

3   He was playing tennis.

   ....

4   She went to school today.

   ....

5   They live here.

   ....

6   She's eating at the moment.

   ....

7   They drove to the station.

   ....

8   She's reading.

   ....

9   He had breakfast early.

   ....

10 They came today.

....

11 She drives to work.

....

12 He left this morning.

....

13 He was writing a letter.

....

14 They watched television.

....

15 She's at home.

....

16 They went home.

....

17 She likes horror films.

....

18 He's walking home.

....

19 They were eating ice cream.

....

20 They gave him the money.

....

84b In your notebook, make ten questions from the box below, and give the answers.

Who	
Why	are you going?
When	did they leave?
Where	is she talking to?
What	did they come here?
What time	are you looking at?
How	did it cost?
How much	

Example: *Why did they leave?*
Because they wanted to catch the train.

85 *Who asked you? Who did you ask?*: question words as subject or object

> *Who* drove the car?
> *Who* did you see?
> *What* happened?
> *What* did you do?

- *who* and *what* are sometimes the subject.
  who and *what* as subject + verb:
  Alison asked *you. Who* asked *you? Alison.*
  NOT ~~Who did ask you?~~

- *who* and *what* are sometimes the object.
  who and *what* as object + question form of verb:
  You asked *Steve. Who* did you ask? *Steve.*

- *Who stayed* **with** *you?*
  but *Who did Jane stay* **with**? (Preposition at the end.)

Practice

Write the questions.

1 Who *came to see* you? Simon came to see me.

2 Who *did Julie meet* last night? Julie met Barbara.

3 What .... you .... reading? I like reading novels.

4 Who ....? Joe made the cake.

5 Who ....? Helen found the car keys.

6 What ....? A cigarette started the fire.

7 What .... you ....? I want some help.

8 Who .... you? Caroline told me.

9 Who .... with Paul? Sue stayed with Paul.

10 What .... you ....? I said nothing.

11 Who ....? David came with Mary.

12 What .... you ....? I study medicine.

13 Who ....? Linda lives with her parents.

14 Who ....? Greg opened the door.

15 What ....? Something terrible happened.

86   Short responses using *so, neither, nor*

- *so* + auxiliary verb + subject is used to say that something which is true about one thing or person is also true about another thing or person:
  '*I can speak Spanish.*'
  '*So can I.*' (= I can speak Spanish too)

- The negative form is ***neither/nor*** + auxiliary verb + subject:
  '*Mike didn't win the prize.*'
  '***Neither**/**Nor** did Bill.*' (= And Bill didn't win it)

- If there is no auxiliary verb in the first sentence, ***do / does / did*** is used:
  '*Leo plays tennis.*'
  '*So does Tom.*'
  '*We went to the cinema last night.*'
  '*So did we.*'

Practice

Write responses to these statements using *So* or *Neither*/*Nor* and the word in brackets.

1   I've got a cold. (I)

   So have I.

2   Peter doesn't eat meat. (Steve)

   Neither/nor does Steve.

3   Sarah had a baby last year. (Jo)

   ....

4   We're going away for the New Year.(we)

   ....

5   I'd like to have a pet. (I)

   ....

6   Harry hasn't finished his essay. (Paul)

   ....

7   I won't be able to go to the meeting. (I)

   ....

8   Jenny could read when she was three. (Fiona)

   ....

9   I wasn't very interested in history when I was at school. (I)

   ....

10 You should do more exercise.(you)

   ....

87   Short responses: *I think so, I hope so*

- ***I think / hope so*** are used to give a positive answer to a question, or to agree with someone without repeating what the other person said:
  'Is it Tuesday today?'
  *'Yes. **I think so.**'* (= I think it is Tuesday)
  'Is it ready?'
  *'**I hope so.**'* (= I hope it's ready)

- The usual negative forms are ***I don't think so***, and ***I hope not***:
  'Will there be many people at the meeting?'
  *'**I don't think so.**'*
  'I think it's going to rain.'
  *'**I hope not.**'*

Practice

Underline the correct or most likely response.

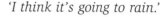

'I think it's going to rain.'

1 'Is Auckland the capital of Australia?'

   a <u>'I don't think so.'</u>   b 'I hope not.'

2 'I think this is going to be a fantastic party.'

   a 'I hope not.'   b <u>'I hope so.'</u>

3 'Will I have to go into hospital?'

   a 'No, I don't think so.'   b 'No, I don't hope so.'

4 'Will the house be finished before next year?

   a 'Yes, I think so.'   b 'Yes, I hope not.'

5 'I think it's going to be sunny this weekend.'

   a 'I think so, because I'm playing tennis on Sunday.'

   b 'I hope so, because I'm playing tennis on Sunday.'

6 'Are there 31 days in July?'

   a 'I hope so.'   b 'I think so.'

7 'I think John's going to give a speech.'

   a 'I hope so. He's really boring.'   b 'I hope not. He's really boring.'

8 'Do you think there will be any food at the party?'

   a 'I don't think so.'   b 'I don't hope so.'

9 'I think we're going to be late.'

   a 'Oh, dear. I think so.'   b 'Oh, dear. I hope not.'

10 'Excuse me? Is there a bank near here?'

   a 'I think so, but I'm not sure.'   b 'I hope so, but I'm not sure.'

RELATIVE CLAUSES

88   Relative clauses with *who* and *that*

- Look at this sentence:
  The man gave me some money.

  If we want to describe the man, we can use an adjective (***old, thin, young,*** etc):
  The old man gave me some money.

- However, sometimes the information we want to give is more complicated.
  The old man met me at the airport. He gave me some money.

  The two sentences can be combined, to show **which** old man gave me
  the money:
  The old man who met me at the airport gave me the money.
  who met me at the airport is a clause (a mini-sentence in the larger
  sentence). It is a called a relative clause because it relates to (= connects
  with) a noun in the larger sentence.

FORM

- Relative clauses are often indicated by ***who*** (for people) and ***that*** (for things
  and sometimes for people). The relative clause is placed immediately after the
  noun which it describes.

  *I was talking to a **person who** worked with my father.*

  *That's the **car that** crashed into our house.*

- *who* or *that* replaces the pronoun:

  I was talking to a person who worked with my father.
  (NOT ~~I was talking to a person who he worked with my father.~~)

  This is the man who I met in Paris.
  (NOT ~~This is the man who I met him in Paris~~)

Practice

88 Join each pair of sentences together to make one sentence, using ***who*** or
that. Write the second sentence as a relative clause.

1   This is the woman. She gave me my first job.

This is the woman who gave me my first job.

2   He picked up the book. It was on the desk.

He picked up the book that was on the desk.

3   The meal was delicious. Ben cooked it.

The meal that Ben cooked was delicious.

4   She's the woman. She telephoned the police.

....

5 He's the person. He wanted to buy your house.

....

6 We threw out the computer. It never worked properly.

....

....

7 This is the lion. It's been ill recently.

....

8 The man was badly injured. He was driving the car.

....

....

9 The children broke my window. They live in the next street.

....

....

10 They sold the cat. It was afraid of mice.

....

11 This is the chair. My parents gave it to me.

....

12 I've applied for the job. You told me about it.

....

13 We're looking for the ball. We were playing with it.

....

....

14 The man was holding the gun. We saw him.

....

15 I'm going to speak to the mechanic. He repaired my car.

....

16 The TV programme was very sad. I watched it last night.

....

....

17 The girl had red hair. I saw her.

....

18 That's the woman. I was telling you about her.

....

Prepositions

PREPOSITIONS OF PLACE

89   *at, in, on*

- *at* is used for a place when the exact position is not very important:

  *He was standing **at** the gate.*
  *We were waiting **at** the station.*

- *on* is used when the place is seen as a line or surface:

  *The cat sat **on** the table.*
  *There was a picture **on** the wall.*

- *in* is used when the place is seen as having volume or area:

  *The dog was **in** the car.*
  *My keys are **in** my bag.*

Practice

Write *at*, *in*, or *on* to complete these sentences.

1   Peter's ..*in*.. the kitchen.

2   The money's .*on*.. the table.

3   He was waiting .*at*.. the station.

4   The milk's .... the fridge.

5   They sat .... the wall.

6   They made the film .... Shepperton Studios.

7   I saw them .... the station.

8   Mary's not here – she's .... the office.

9   They were sitting .... the floor.

10 The butter's .... the shelf .... the cupboard.

11 The money's .... my pocket.

12 They are all .... the garden.

13 The papers are .... my desk.

14 They are all .... the car.

15 He's not .... work today – he's .... home.

90 Prepositions of movement

- *to*, *at*, or *away from* a place

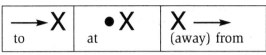

She ran *to* the gate.
She stood *at* the gate.
She walked *away from* the gate.

- *on, onto*, or *off* a line or surface (a wall, table, floor, etc)

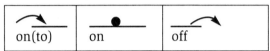

I *put the money onto the table.*
The money's *on* the table.
The money fell *off* the table.

- *in*, *into*, or *out of* a box, car, or anything with volume

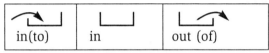

The dog jumped *into* the car.
The dog's *in* the car.
Take the dog *out of* the car.

Practice

Choose the correct words from the boxes to complete these sentences.

1 She was standing .*at*.. the front door.

2 I put the matches .... the table.

3 She got .... the car and ran .... the station.

4 The baby's going to fall .... the table.

5 The bread's .... the cupboard.

6 I walked .... the church and waited .... the bus stop.

7 He was lying .... the floor.

8 She dived .... the sea.

9 They climbed .... the roof and looked down at us.

10 We walked .... the end of the road.

91 Prepositions of position and movement

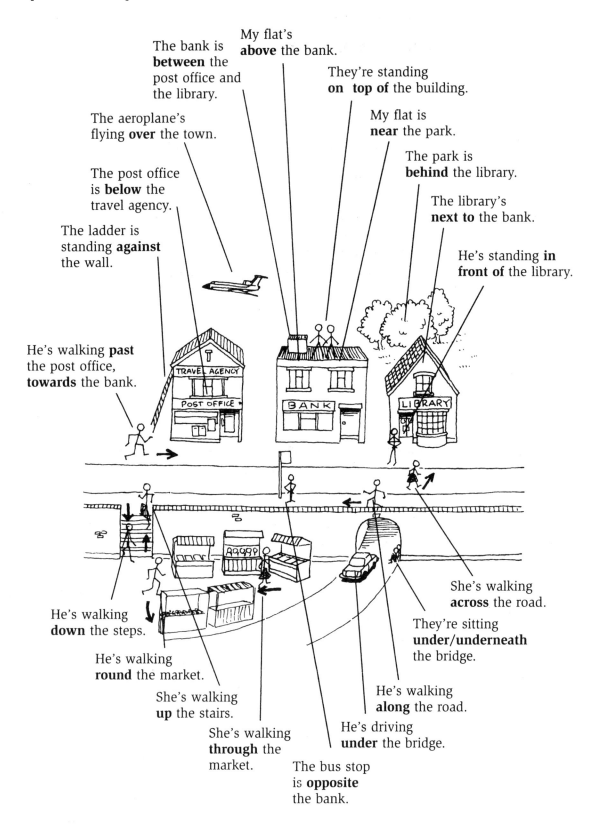

The bank is **between** the post office and the library.

My flat's **above** the bank.

They're standing **on top of** the building.

The aeroplane's flying **over** the town.

My flat is **near** the park.

The post office is **below** the travel agency.

The park is **behind** the library.

The ladder is standing **against** the wall.

The library's **next to** the bank.

He's standing **in front of** the library.

He's walking **past** the post office, **towards** the bank.

She's walking **across** the road.

He's walking **down** the steps.

They're sitting **under/underneath** the bridge.

He's walking **round** the market.

He's walking **along** the road.

She's walking **up** the stairs.

He's driving **under** the bridge.

She's walking **through** the market.

The bus stop is **opposite** the bank.

- Some prepositions indicate movement.
  *I ran **past** the school.*
  *He walked **through** the gate.*

- Some prepositions indicate position:
  *The bank is **next to** the post office.*
  *My house is **opposite** the school.*

- Some prepositions can indicate movement or position:
  *We drove **under** the bridge.*
  *They were standing **under** the bridge.*

Practice

Write these sentences, choosing the correct word.

1 They ran (*across/opposite*) the road.

   They ran across the road.

2 We had a picnic on the hill (*over/above*) the village.

   ....

3 I put the ladder (*against/up*) the wall.

   ....

4 The snake moved quietly (*through/across*) the tall grass.

   ....

5 The mouse ran quickly (*across/through*) the path.

   ....

6 The cat walked slowly (*on top of/along*) the wall.

   ....

7 We sat (*on top of/along*) the cliffs and watched the sea.

   ....

8 Someone pushed a letter (*under/below*) the door.

   ....

9 She drove (*between/through*) the gates.

   ....

10 I held the parcel (*behind/past*) my back.

   ....

11 They walked (*in front of/past*) the school gate.

   ....

12 I pushed my bike (*over/above*) the bridge.

   ....

13 The bank clerk stood (*against/towards*) the wall.

....

14 We waited (*down/under*) a tree.

....

15 I put my suitcase (*on top of/over*) the wardrobe.

....

92 Prepositions of position and movement

Check

Use the most suitable prepositions from Exercises 89, 90, and 91 to complete these sentences. Sometimes more than one answer is possible.

1 The dog ran ..*round*.. the tree five or six times.

2 We flew slowly .... the suburbs of Paris.

3 I moved the baby .... the fire.

4 The police ran .... the crowd and arrested a young man.

5 If you put some money .... here, the machine will start.

6 They had nowhere to stay so they slept .... a bridge.

7 The town hall is .... the library and the museum.

8 We watched the soldiers as they walked .... our house on their way to the ship.

9 They ran out of the dressing-room .... the football pitch.

10 London is .... the south-east of England.

11 The dog stood .... the door and waited.

12 They walked hand-in-hand .... the side of the canal.

13 I didn't want my mother to see her present, so I held it .... my back.

14 The cat jumped .... my arms and ran away.

15 I threw the stone .... the sea.

16 The bottles fell .... the lorry and rolled .... the hill.

17 It was too dark to see so he walked slowly, holding his arms .... him.

18 I put a chair .... the door to stop anyone coming in.

19 We crawled .... a hole in the fence.

20 What have you got .... your hand?

21 The cat was sitting .... the cupboard, looking down at me.

22 I was frightened. I could see him walking .... me, with a very angry look on his face.

23 I tied the string .... my waist.

24 If you are feeling sick, you should sit .... a chair and put you head .... your knees.

25 The cat jumped out of the tree .... the roof of my car.

93 Certain verbs with *to* or *at*

- Some verbs are followed by *to* or *at*, and some verbs do not use a preposition:
  Listen to *me!*
  Look at *me!*
  She **told** *me the news.*

Practice

Write *to*, *at* or nothing to complete these sentences.

1 I sent the parcel ..to.. her yesterday.

2 Are you going to phone .... your parents now?

3 What did you say .... them?

4 The children were terrified when he shouted .... them.

5 What did you tell .... them?

6 I took the box out of my pocket and gave it .... her.

7 We explained the problem .... the attendant.

8 I don't know why they were laughing .... us.

9 She caught the ball and threw it gently back .... me.

10 They were arrested for throwing stones .... the police.

PREPOSITIONS OF TIME

94   *at, in, on*

- *at* a point in time:
  at four o'clock, *at* bedtime

- *on* a day or date:
  on Monday, *on* July 6th, *on* your birthday

- *in* a period of time:
  in the morning, *in* April, *in* the summer, *in* 1987

Notes

- *at* night, *at* Christmas, *at* Easter
- *on* Monday, *in* the morning, *on* Monday morning

Practice

Write *at*, *in* or *on* to complete these sentences.

1 I'll see you .*on*.. Monday.

2 I met him .... the holidays.

3 I'll pick you up .... eight o'clock.

4 I'm going home .... four.

5 They came to visit us .... my birthday.

6 I can work .... the morning but I don't like working .... night.

7 Did you have a good time .... Christmas?

8 School finishes .... three o'clock .... Thursdays.

9 We arranged to meet .... seven .... the morning.

10 We had a party .... the last day of the course.

11 I often go skiing .... winter.

12 What time do you get back .... Tuesday?

13 She's going to visit her parents .... Easter.

14 He was born .... 8th June 1968.

15 Stuart can come and see you .... lunchtime.

16 I always send my wife flowers .... our wedding anniversary.

17 The conference is .... July.

95 *until*

> *Our friends are staying with us **until** Sunday.* (= They are leaving on Sunday.)
> *Our friends stayed with us **until** Sunday.* (= They left on Sunday.)

- ***until*** + the end of a period of time (past or future)

- After ***until*** we can use a time word or expression, e.g. ***until*** *Monday,* ***until*** *the end of the week,* or we can use a clause with a subject and verb, e.g. ***until*** *I had children,* ***until*** *this programme finishes.*

- ***until*** + present simple to talk about the future:
  *I'm going to watch television **until** this programme finishes.*

- ***until*** is often shortened to ***till*** in spoken English.

Practice

Rewrite the sentences, using ***until***.

1   We stayed at the party and we left at midnight.
    We stayed at the party until midnight.

2   I'm watching this game. I'm going to stop watching it when it finishes.
    I'm going to watch this game until it finishes.

3   They played on the beach. They stopped playing when it got dark.
    ....

4   Wait. Stop waiting when the bus stops.
    ....

5   I'm going to stay in bed. I'm going to get up a 11 o'clock.
    ....

6   We're looking round the shops. We're going to stop looking round when the rain stops.
    ....

7   I lived by the sea. I moved away from there when I was fifteen.
    ....

8   I drove. I stopped driving when we got to London.
    ....

9   You should lie down. You should get up when you feel better.
    ....

10 I'm in the office. I'm going to leave here at 6 o'clock.
    ....

96 *until, before, after*

- *before* and *after* can be followed by a noun, pronoun, clause or gerund:
  *I'll see you **after** lunch.*
  *John arrived **before** me.*
  *She phoned **after** the party started.*
  *We had some coffee **before** starting the meeting.*

Check

96a Join the sentences with *before* or *until*.

1 I should stay here. The snow stops.

   I should stay here until the snow stops.

2 I learnt to speak some Turkish. I went to Turkey.

   I learnt to speak some Turkish before I went to Turkey.

3 They stayed awake. Their daughter came home.

   ....

4 I'm going to stay here. It's time to go home.

   ....

5 I'm going to finish working. I'm sixty.

   ....

6 The meeting started. I arrived.

   ....

7 We waited. The ambulance came.

   ....

8 Are you going to carry on working at the cafe? You can find a better job.

   ....

9 I'd like to visit the Acropolis. I leave Greece.

   ....

10 He usually has a big breakfast. He goes to work.

   ....

96b In your notebook, join the phrases in the two columns using **until**, **before** or **after** to make eleven sentences.

~~1 You must stay in bed~~	a my exams start
~~2 I felt very tired~~	~~b staying awake all night~~
3 I was asleep	c it gets too dark
4 We always have a good breakfast	d he was thirty
5 We're going to buy some new skis	~~e you get better~~
6 They felt lonely	f we go on our skiing holiday
7 I have a lot of studying to do	g we go to work
8 Who's going to wash the dishes	h the phone work me up
9 He lived with his parents	i I found it
10 I carried on looking for my ring	j dinner
11 We must walk home	k their children left home

Examples: 1 *You must stay in bed until you get better.* *1e*

2 *I felt very tired after staying awake all night.* *2b*

97 Prepositions of time

Practice

Use one of these words to complete the sentences below.

until	during	after	before
through	between	from	in

1 I waited _until_ nine o'clock and then went home.

2 If you come .... seven, we'll catch the bus that leaves at 7.05.

3 Will you come and see me .... a week or two?

4 .... the children left, the house was very quiet.

5 .... the holidays, we played tennis and did a lot of swimming.

6 I can't remember when we left the cinema: I think it was .... ten and half-past.

7 I was ill .... January to March.

8 We worked all .... the holidays to finish painting the boat.

Phrasal Verbs

- A phrasal verb is formed when a preposition (**up, down, in,** etc) or an adverb (**away, back,** etc) is added to a verb to produce a new verb with a different meaning:

  *I **get up** at eight o'clock.*

  *We'll **pick** you **up** outside the station.*

  *The plane **took off** very quickly.*

- The meaning of a phrasal verb can be similar to the original verb:

  *The car **slowed down** and then stopped.* (= similar meaning to slow)

  – or it can be completely different to the original:
  *I'm going to **give up** smoking.* (= different meaning to **give**)

98   Some common phrasal verbs

Practice

wake up	look after	ring up
~~get up~~	sit down	get on
stand up	give up	

Choose the correct phrasal verbs from the list above to complete these sentences.

1   The children ..*get up*.. at eight o'clock to have breakfast.

2   '......................!' he said. 'This is not the time for sleeping!'

3   After the crash, my legs hurt: it was very difficult to ....

4   '...................... in that chair, please,' said the doctor.

5   The bus was moving too fast and I couldn't .... it.

6   Mr and Mrs Smith are going to .... the children for an hour.

7   I'm going to .... smoking tomorrow.

8   I'm going to .... the station and ask about the trains.

99 More phrasal verbs

Practice

99a Read the dialogue and underline the phrasal verbs. Write each phrasal verb in the infinitive in your notebook.

A: Oh hello. Nice to see you again. Did you have a good holiday? I was planning to <u>ring</u> you <u>up</u> to ask you about it.

B: Yes, it was lovely. We had to <u>set off</u> really early because the plane took off at 6 a.m. But then we were on the beach in the sun by lunch time.

A: Great! And what did you do most days?

B: Well, we usually slept in. It was very nice not having to get up early. And then we stayed up late at night, going out to discos and nightclubs. During the day, we usually lay on the beach or looked round the town.

A: And what about food?

B: Well, we didn't usually have any breakfast. By the time we got down stairs at the hotel, they had cleared away all the breakfast things. We tried out different restaurants for lunch and most of them were very good. The fish was particularly nice. And we usually stayed in for dinner at the hotel.

A: So what did you like best?

B: I liked everything – the beaches, the weather, the food, the night life, the people. I'd like to go back again next year so I'm saving up for it already. People book very early for that area so I must fix it up after the New Year. If I carry on saving for a few months, I'll have enough money.

99b Match the phrasal verbs from exercise 99a with these definitions. Copy the definitions with the correct phrasal verb into your notebook.

1 To test something for the first time to find out whether it is good or not.
   = *try out*

2 To rise into the air to start flying (usually a plane or a bird). = *take off*

3 To make the arrangements for something. ....

4 To visit a place and look at the different parts of it. ....

5 To stay inside somewhere, not to go out. ....

6 To begin a journey. ....

7 To make somewhere tidy by removing things (e.g. plates and food from a table, toys from a floor). ....

8 To continue to do something. ....

9 To get out of bed. ....

10 To return. ....

11 To not be in bed late at night, after bedtime. ....

12 To not spend some of your money, but to put it away or in a bank.

   ....

13 To leave the house/hotel to go somewhere, usually for pleasure.

   ....

14 To sleep late in the morning. ....

15 To telephone someone. ....

100 Phrasal verbs that don't take an object

> The car **broke down** on the way to hospital and we had to call for an ambulance.
>
> Please **hurry up**! We're going to miss the train.
>
> **Look out**! There's a car coming.

- Like other verbs, some phrasal verbs take an object:

  Can you **pick up**   **that bag?**

              verb   object

  And some phrasal verbs do not take an object:

  We **'re setting off** (no object) *at 7 o'clock tomorrow morning.*

        verb

- Examples of phrasal verbs that don't take an object:

  to break down = to stop working (when talking about machinery)
  to hurry up = to move, go, do something faster
  to look out = to take care

Practice

Complete the sentences, using the phrasal verbs in the box. Put the verbs into the correct tense and form.

get up	break down	set off	sleep in	stay in
speak up	go back	hurry up	go out	look out

1   My washing machine ..*broke down*.. this morning so I had to do all the washing by hand.

2   The train leaves at 5.45 so I think we should .... at 5.00.

3   I'd like to .... tonight but I've got a lot of work to do so I should ....

4   Please .... We're going to be late.

5   Oh good. I don't have to .... early for work tomorrow so I can ....

6   I'm sorry but my hearing is not very good. Could you please ....?

7   ....! You're going to hit that car.

8   I had a holiday in Malaysia last year and it was beautiful. I'd love to ....

101   Phrasal verbs that take an object: separable

> I **looked up** the new words in a dictionary.
>
> Can you **put away** the dishes?
>
> I **put** my glasses **down** somewhere but I can't remember where.
>
> They've got too much money; they should **give** some of it **away**.
>
> I don't know the answer but I must **find** it **out**.

- Many phrasal verbs take an object: *I can't **pick up** this bag.*

- We can say:

  I can't | *pick   up* | | *this bag.* | or
          verb particle   object

  I can't | *pick* | | *this bag* | | *up.*
          verb   object particle

The verb and the particle can separate. The particle can go before or after the object.

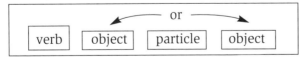

- If the object is a pronoun (**her, me, it,** etc.) it goes **before** the particle:

  *I can't **pick** it **up**.*

  NOT ~~I can't pick up it.~~

- Examples of phrasal verbs that take an object (separable):

to look up = to find the meaning of a word in a dictionary or to find some other information in a book

to put away = to put something in its proper place, e.g. a cupboard or box

to put down = to put something on a surface, e.g. a table or the floor

to give away = to give something to someone free of charge

to find out = to find information about something

to turn on = to start a machine by putting electricity into it

to turn off = to stop a machine by stopping the supply of electricity

to work out = to solve a problem by thinking hard about it

to put off = to delay something to a later date

Practice

In your notebook, rewrite the sentences substituting the underlined words with a phrasal verb from the box. Write the sentences
a) with the object after the verb and particle;
b) with the object between the verb and particle.
(Where the object is a pronoun, you can only put it between the verb and particle.)

look up	fix up	give away	turn on	turn off
put down	ring up	put away	work out	put off

1 I usually <u>telephone</u> my sister at the weekend for a chat.

   I usually ring up my sister at the weekend for a chat.

   I usually ring my sister up at the weekend for a chat.

2 These clothes are too small for Andrew. I should <u>give</u> them <u>to someone else.</u>

3 I don't know the meaning of this word. I must <u>find</u> it <u>in the dictionary</u>.

4 We should talk about this problem. Can we <u>arrange</u> a meeting?

5 Your room looks terrible, James. Why don't you <u>put</u> your clothes <u>into the cupboard</u>.

6 Would you like to <u>put</u> your bag <u>on the floor</u>?

7 This problem is really difficult. Could you help me <u>solve</u> it?

8 OK, we're ready. Would you <u>start</u> the machine, please?

9 Marie can't come. She wants to <u>delay</u> the meeting until Monday.

10 The machine is too noisy. Could you <u>stop</u> it <u>working</u>, please?

102 Phrasal verbs that take an object but do not separate

> She was very ill last year but she has **got over** the illness now.
>
> He **takes after** his father. He's got the same blonde hair and blue eyes and the same gentle manner.
>
> She works in the mornings but she can't **live off** that. She must find a full-time job.
>
> I **came across** an old photograph of you yesterday. It was taken when you were at school.

- Some phrasal verbs do not have the object between the verb and the particle. In these verbs, the verb and the particle cannot separate. They are **inseparable**. The object can only go after the verb and the particle:

  *I'd like to go out tonight. Can you **look after** the children? (**to look after** = to take care of someone or something)*

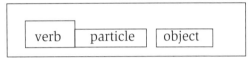

We cannot say: *Can you look the children after?*

- When the object is a pronoun, it goes after the phrasal verb in the same way: *Can you **look after** them?*

- Examples of phrasal verbs that take an object but do not separate:

  ***to get over** = to recover from something, e.g. an illness, the death of a relative or friend, etc. That is, to get better after something bad happens to you*

  ***to take after** = to look or behave like a parent (or older relative)*

  ***to live off** = to get money from something to pay for everything you need to live, e.g. food, clothes, transport, etc.*

  ***to come across** = to find something or meet someone by chance*

102 Practice

Complete the sentences with a verb from the box. Put the verb into the correct tense form.

take after	come across	live on
look round	~~get over~~	look after

1 He was very unhappy after his girlfriend left him but I think he is

   starting to *get over* it now.

2 We're going on holiday next month. We must find someone to

   .... the cat and the plants.

3 I know you've seen the new part of the town but you should

   .... the old part – it's very interesting.

4   We were on our way to college when we ……………………… some

dancers. They were doing a beautiful dance in the street.

5   He's very good at sport and his mother is, too. He ………………………

her.

6   She loves acting but she can't ……………………… the money she earns

from it. She has to do other jobs.

Test 1

Part A

Circle the correct words to complete the sentences

1 I talked to (*he/him*) yesterday.

2 I cut (*me/myself*) when I was shaving.

3 I hope you enjoyed (*yourself/you*) today.

4 Do you like (*your/yours*) new teacher?

5 I think that table is (*our/ours*).

6 The company has decided to move (*it's/its*) main office.

7 Mark won the (*men's/mens'*) swimming championship last year.

8 Are you going to the (*engineer's/engineers'*) conference?

9 Have they sent (*we/us*) an invitation?

10 If you can't find the book, you can borrow (*my/mine*).

SCORING

10 points: *Give yourself a point for each correct answer.*   Score ☐

Part B

Write *a/an*, *the*, *some*, or *any* to complete these sentences.

1 I'm reading .... very interesting book at the moment.

2 I'd like .... information about your language course, please.

3 Could you answer .... telephone, please?

4 There weren't .... letters for you this morning.

5 Would you .... like coffee?

6 Are there .... good restaurants near here?

7 I'd love to be .... astronaut.

8 Maurizio plays .... piano really well.

9 They were the first people to fly non-stop round .... world in a balloon.

10 Listen! I've got .... good news for you.

SCORING

10 points: *Give yourself a point for each correct answer.*   Score ☐

Part C

Write **a/an** or **the** if necessary.

My sister Claire lives in ¹................ small stone house in ²................ village in ³................ Scotland. ⁴................ house is quite old, and it has ⁵................ beautiful view of ⁶................ sea. Claire is ⁷................ writer, so she is able to work at ⁸................ home. Her husband Ian teaches ⁹................ philosophy at ¹⁰................ Edinburgh University, which is ¹⁰................ oldest university in Scotland. Ian comes from ¹²................ USA, and they usually go there once ¹³................ year to visit his family. Claire and Ian have ¹⁴................ daughter, Jessica, who is not yet old enough to go to ¹⁵................ school.

SCORING

15 points: *Give yourself a point for each correct answer.*   Score ☐

Part D

Find the mistake in each sentence and rewrite the sentence correctly.

1   There are a lot people in the street.

    ....

2   Anyone's stolen my wallet!

    ....

3   Hurry up! We haven't got many time.

    ....

4   Are you more tall than I am?

    ....

5   If I take that job, I'll have fewer money but more time.

    ....

    ....

6   My new manager is friendlier the old one.

    ....

7   This summer is hotter as last summer.

    ....

8   Which is highest mountain in your country?

....

9   This test isn't as difficult the last one we did.

....

....

10 We were too tired get to the top of the mountain.

....

....

11 That film was really bored.

....

12 Well done! You have all worked very hardly.

....

13 Please could you drive more careful?

....

14 Have you finished your journey, or do you have to travel more far?

....

....

15 This is the worse road in the country.

....

SCORING

15 points: *Give yourself a point for each correct answer*   Score ☐

TOTAL SCORE

Maximum 50 points. *Add up your score.*   Total Score ☐

Test 2

Part A

Circle the correct words to complete the sentences.

1 Most mornings, I (*get up/am getting up*) at 6.30.

2 Where (*do you work/are you working*) at the moment?

3 I don't understand what this word (*means/is meaning*).

4 Who (*you saw/did you see*) at the conference last week?

5 The taxi (*arrives/arrived*) five minutes ago.

6 I (*lived/have lived*) in Brazil since 1998.

7 We've been waiting for you (*for/since*) half an hour.

8 Look at that plane! It (*will/is going*) to crash.

9 The letters (*are/were*) posted yesterday.

10 She (*uses/used*) to be a dancer, but now she works in a bank.

SCORING

10 points: *Give yourself a point for each correct answer.*   Score ☐

Part B

Complete the short answers.

1 Are you going to the concert?   Yes, ...

2 Does your father know about this?   No, ...

3 Is you sister learning Spanish?   Yes, ...

4 Do I write clearly enough?   Yes, ...

5 Was the sun shining when you left home?   No, ...

6 Did the students enjoy the lecture?   Yes, ...

7 Were the cats fighting when you got up?   Yes, ...

8 Am I seeing the dentist tomorrow?   No, ...

9 Are you and Jo moving house?   Yes, ...

10 Did you hear about Tom?   No, ...

SCORING

10 points: *Give yourself a point for each correct answer.*   Score ☐

Part C

Complete the conversation on a separate sheet of paper, putting the verbs into the correct tense and form and adding all the other words you need.

ANDY: Hello, Liz. I / not / see / you / a long time. How / you?
LIZ: Fine, thanks. What about you? What / you / do / these days?
ANDY: At / moment / I work / my parents' restaurant, but yesterday I / have / job / interview with a law firm.
LIZ: Great! How / it / go? /
ANDY: Well, unfortunately, I / a little late.
LIZ: Why?
ANDY: Well, my watch / steal / last week, when / I swim.
LIZ: Oh, dear. And / they / ask / you / many difficult questions?
ANDY: Yes, but I / think I / do / OK.
LIZ: So / they / offer you / job?
ANDY: I / not / hear / yet. They / tell me tomorrow.
LIZ: Well, good luck.

SCORING

20 points. *Take off a point for each mistake.*   Score ☐

Part D

Put the verbs in brackets into the correct tense and form to complete the sentences.

1 I'm afraid I can't come to your party. My boss .... to dinner. (come)

2 The plane .... too low when it crashed into a mountain. (fly)

3 Simon is a journalist now, but he .... an athlete. (be)

4 .... for me! (not/wait)

5 Coffee .... in the mountains. (grow)

6 .... the report yet? (you/finish)

7 Goodbye. I .... you tomorrow. (see)

8 I .... for twelve hours last night. (sleep)

9 We .... a new car. (just/buy)

10 The new Pope .... yesterday. (choose)

SCORING

10 points: *Give yourself a point for each correct answer.*   Score ☐

TOTAL SCORE

Maximum 50 points. *Add up your score.*   Total Score ☐

Test 3

Part A

Circle the correct words to complete the sentences.

1 She (*won't/wouldn't*) have all these problems if she was more efficient.

2 If it (*rains/rained*), we'll go by bus.

3 Where (*will/would*) you live if you could choose?

4 The boss always (*gets/got*) angry if people are late for work.

5 Felipe (*can't/couldn't*) speak any English when I first met him.

6 You look tired. You (*might/should*) go to bed.

7 (*Must/Can*) you close the door, please?

8 I think it (*can/may*) rain tomorrow.

9 Our car broke down so we (*had to/must*) take a taxi.

10 You (*don't have to/mustn't*) tell anyone – it's a secret.

SCORING

10 points: *Give yourself a point for each correct answer.*   Score ☐

Part B

Put the verb into either the gerund or the infinitive with **to** form.

1 Do you enjoy .... ? (cook)

2 I've decided .... a new job. (look for)

3 Are you interested in .... this report? (read)

4 He borrowed my camera without .... me. (ask)

5 I've bought this new suit .... for my interview. (wear)

6 .... is a very exciting sport. (ski)

7 You have to take an exam .... the course. (pass)

8 Thank you for .... us to your party. (invite)

9 Have they finished .... the new road? (build)

10 The children refused .... to bed. (go)

SCORING

10 points: *Give yourself a point for each correct answer.*   Score ☐

Part C

Write these sentences in reported speech, using the words in brackets. Change tenses and pronouns where necessary.

1 'I will look at the car this afternoon.' (The mechanic says)

....

2 'I'm a dentist.' (She said)

....

3 'We aren't going to sell our house.' (They say)

....

4 'Your passport is out of date, Mr Smith.' (The officer told)

....

5 'I'm waiting to see the doctor.' (The woman said)

....

6 'I love you, Anna.' (He told)

....

7 'My mother's coming to see me.' (Mary says)

....

8 I'm looking for my sister.' (The boy said)

....

9 'You play the piano very well, Leo.' (The teacher told)

....

10 'We're having a wonderful holiday.' (They said)

....

SCORING

10 points: *Give yourself a point for each correct answer.*   Score ☐

Part D

Find the mistake in each sentence and rewrite the sentence correctly.

1   Have you given to your friend the money?

....

2   We go often to the beach in the summer.

....

3   I took an umbrella so it was raining.

....

4   Both Jenny and Sue don't have the right qualifications.

....

5   Like you fishing?

....

6   Why they did leave?

....

7   'I don't like doing tests.' 'Nor I don't.'

....

....

8   'Is he going to give a long speech?' 'I don't hope so.'

....

....

9   That's the woman who she has just started working here.

....

10 These are the earrings that my aunt bought them for me.

....

SCORING

10 points: *Give yourself a point for each correct answer.*   Score ☐

Part E

Complete the sentences with a preposition or adverb.

1 The man walked .... the hotel and asked the receptionist for a room.

2 We were waiting .... the bus stop.

3 Let's meet .... 9 o'clock.

4 I'll wait .... you're ready.

5 Have you given .... smoking?

6 Everyone laughs .... him because he's so stupid.

7 Can you look .... the children for me while I go to the shops?

8 I always feel nervous when the plane takes ....

9 I'm really tired. Do you think I could sit .... ?

10 If you don't go to bed now, then you won't be able to get .... in the morning.

SCORING
10 points: *Give yourself a point for each correct answer.*   Score ☐

TOTAL SCORE
Maximum 50 points. *Add up your score.*   Total Score ☐

Index

Note that all numbers in this index are page numbers.